## Reviews of *Who Scooped My Bagel?*

*"Everyone has a story, but not everyone has the courage
to tell it. Mary Beall Adler has that courage."*

*"Mary's story rings true because she is honest and authentic.
By making herself vulnerable, she charms the reader and makes this
book a must-read for everyone who mixes some amount of wishful
thinking with practicality. That would be just about all of us!"*

*"Mary paints a wonderful story with well-chosen words.
I love her ability to handle cranky kids and grumpy adults
with magic bagel wands and a big dose of humor."*

*"The stories in this book are memorable—from a do-it-yourself
burger guy to a lady who wants bagels without holes. The author
thoughtfully explains the baking process, the history of the bagel,
and her own personal story. I am buying copies for all my friends."*

*"Such a delightful read! This is a book to enjoy and savor.
No doubt you'll rush out to buy some freshly baked bagels to nosh
on while you devour Mary Beall Adler's insp͏ g words."*

T01Ɖ6869

# WHO SCOOPED MY BAGEL?

One Woman's Story
of Love, Loss and Success

MARY BEALL ADLER

Published by Advantage, Charleston, South Carolina.
Member of Advantage Media Group.

ADVANTAGE is a registered trademark and the Advantage colophon is a trademark of Advantage Media Group, Inc.

Printed in the United States of America.

ISBN: 978-1-59932-382-4
LCCN: 2013935139

This publication is designed to provide accurate and authoritative information in regard to the subject matter covered. It is sold with the understanding that the publisher is not engaged in rendering legal, accounting, or other professional services. If legal advice or other expert assistance is required, the services of a competent professional person should be sought.

Advantage Media Group is proud to be a part of the Tree Neutral® program. Tree Neutral offsets the number of trees consumed in the production and printing of this book by taking proactive steps such as planting trees in direct proportion to the number of trees used to print books. To learn more about Tree Neutral, please visit www.treeneutral.com. To learn more about Advantage's commitment to being a responsible steward of the environment, please visit www.advantagefamily.com/green

Advantage Media Group is a publisher of business, self-improvement, and professional development books and online learning. We help entrepreneurs, business leaders, and professionals share their Stories, Passion, and Knowledge to help others Learn & Grow. Do you have a manuscript or book idea that you would like us to consider for publishing? Please visit advantagefamily.com or call 1.866.775.1696.

*With heartfelt love to*
*all my brothers and sisters, actual and extended;*
*Jonathan Adler;*
*Sunny and Warren Adler;*
*and my children*

# Acknowledgments

I wanted to write this book in order to share my creativity and success in the traditional bagel business. I made many mistakes, of course, both personal and professional. However, I managed to turn errors into learning experiences and to ensure that my business would thrive by making corrections to style and operations.

It is important for me to participate in something I love every day. Luckily, the bagel business is something I love. My other love, writing, gives me the chance to touch readers and to share my experiences.

I wish to thank my husband and children for allowing me time to write this book, even when that meant something else had to wait. We synced our calendars daily, and I lived constantly with my iPhone. In many ways, life is a juggling act. I made time for writing about my personal journey.

Many thanks to Leslie Atkins for her insightful writing assistance. This book benefitted greatly from her talents and intelligence. In the process of working together, we became good friends.

# Contents

# Introduction

*I wish everyone could smell a bagel bakery at 3:00 a.m. The smell of freshly baked, hot bagels is comforting. The scent of warm yeast rising mixes with the aromas of rye, cinnamon, salt, poppy seeds, onions, and raisins.*

*I am in the bakery business. Some people call me the "bagel lady," and that moniker sticks. But there's so much more to the story…*

# Chapter 1:
# THE WARMTH OF A BAGEL BAKERY

*Laughter is brightest where food is best.*

—IRISH PROVERB

In the bagel business, I have learned that a bagel can be a metaphor for life: some of us feel as if what surrounds us is different from what is inside. I have faced my share of difficulties and learned along the way to develop a strong crust on the outside while retaining softness inside my heart and spirit. Just like my bagels.

I have cracked thousands of eggs in my life. I have cracked them one at a time using both hands, one at a time using one hand, two at a time using two hands, three at a time (one in one hand and two in the other), and four at a time (two in each hand). The particular technique depends on my mood and what I am making.

Naturally, I often identify my egg-related experiences with whatever is happening in my life at the time. I usually try to make an analogy between each of those moments and the act of cracking an egg.

If one piece of a shell gets mixed and blended in with five pounds of eggs, typically the addition of that one tiny bit of shell goes unnoticed. In my experience, the bigger the mix, the less important the little shells are; they can always be siphoned or scooped out.

It is not as easy to get rid of the bits of pain in our personal lives, whether they are in large pieces or tiny nagging ones.

Of course, too many shells in a mix does not constitute a recipe for success—personal or otherwise.

## How It All Started

I came to Washington, D.C., one summer while I was waiting for the next term to begin at Antioch Law School (I had late admittance). As I was walking around the law school's upscale Georgetown neighborhood, I discovered a bagel shop along the commercial corridor, on M Street.

I love bagels, so I returned to the shop over and over. It was where I ate my breakfast and lunch almost daily. The shop was lively, and the owner—a big guy with a seemingly big heart— intrigued me. He talked to his customers about everything from global news to artistic life. He was interesting and exuded passion.

I was fascinated to learn that he had been an English Literature major and played football at Cornell University—quite a dichotomy. In Ithaca, he had learned to bake bagels while working at a part-time job. He had left Cornell for the University of Vermont where he had continued to bake bread and studied classical music. He played the flute.

Every time I went into the bagel shop, Razz would drop whatever he was doing in the back and come up to the counter to wait on me. He always remembered what I liked, and he always commented on whatever book I had with me. This made me nervous, but I liked him. Razz looked exotic; he had a French-Jamaican mother and a Danish father.

Razz was always covered in flour. He had hard-working, calloused hands; kind eyes; and a huge smile. We talked about books and music. He found out I had been a gymnast, so he asked me to go running with him along the C&O Canal. One day, he came into the store where I was working and brought me piano sheet music. I was charmed.

On our first official date, Razz invited me to a rehearsal of his quintet. When I heard him play the flute, I fell in love. It was a magical, mesmerizing evening. I listened to him and his friends make musical vibrations that slipped over the balcony and echoed across the Potomac River below.

Afterwards, we went to a restaurant where Razz knew the chef, and we were treated like royalty. We ate and talked, but did not stay long; Razz made sure we left quickly, since he had to get up early for the morning bake.

Razz never let anyone get close emotionally, but I did not absorb that fact until much later. Our conversations were often superficial because he would shut down and turn to intellect rather than his heart. Perhaps even now I am glamorizing it, but this was how it seemed to me.

That fall, I started attending Antioch Law School, which was located about a mile north of the White House. Antioch's students, who were generally older, usually came to the law after working in other professions. Many of us had strong moral convictions and wanted to help society by representing impoverished people.

Personally, I was intent on studying poverty law and women's rights. I even worked on an internship with a battered women's shelter. I enjoyed tax law, too. Unfortunately, that would come in handy much later. But I am getting ahead of myself.

Part of the law school curriculum dictated that we students were supposed to live in the kinds of environments in which our clients lived, so we would better understand where they came from and how their life experiences impacted their situations.

I rented the fourth floor of a family brownstone in a rough section of downtown D.C. Back in those days, the neighborhood was not safe at all. I saw drug dealers out and about on the street, and I heard gunshots regularly at night. After my initial shock, though, I grew used to the continual sirens and sights of inner city life.

Law school was expensive. I had to work hard and be creative to support myself. I took out several student loans. Soon, I noticed that there was not a convenient place to eat either at school or near the law library. I began getting up at 4:00 a.m. to make sandwiches, which I sold in the tiny basement lounge where law students communed between classes.

I bought ingredients from the grocery store and began making ten sandwiches a day. They immediately sold out. Within a week, I was selling fifty sandwiches a day, which translated into a $100 profit each day.

Razz offered to sell me bagels at his wholesale price, so I added bagels to the menu. Soon I was selling five dozen bagels with cream cheese daily. I limited my selling time to an hour and a half so it would not cut into study time.

Even on this limited schedule, I was making more than $200 dollars a day, five days a week. My professors commented that I would probably end up in business because I had an entrepreneurial flair. At that point, I still believed I would become a lawyer, so I dismissed their comments.

I became fairly well known for selling bagels in law school. Everyone started to call me "The Bagel Lady." The nickname has lasted, even to this day.

> *Everyone started to call me "The Bagel Lady." The nickname has lasted, even to this day.*

## The History of Bagels

Like much of history, the bagel's culinary origin is a mixture of fact and rumor. The bagel-baking tradition originated in Eastern Europe in the early 1600s. Originally made of white flour, bagels were considered great delicacies in Eastern Europe, where poor people generally ate only black bread (usually made of rye or barley).

In the 1800s, the bagel tradition came along with waves of Jewish immigrants to the United States, Canada, and the United Kingdom, finding homes in in New York City, Montreal, and London's Brick Lane district.

Like many other foods in immigrant-rich New York City, bagels became rooted in the American psyche. While still a Jewish delicacy most often eaten with cream cheese, bagels became popular in society in general.

The popularity of adding lox (thinly sliced smoked salmon) to bagels supposedly started when barrels of salted salmon were shipped from the West Coast to the East Coast via the newly completed transcontinental railroad.

Experts tend to believe that the word *bagel* originates with the Yiddish word *beigen*, which means "to bend."

Bagels may be cousins of pretzels, which were staples among Jewish bakers in Germany prior to their migration into Poland during the Middle Ages.

### BAGEL WISDOM

**CONGRATULATIONS. IT'S A BAGEL:** According to one story, Jewish women received bagels as gifts when they gave birth. According to another, Jewish families would eat bagels on Saturday nights after their Sabbath was over. Since Jewish law dictates that no cooking is allowed until the sundown after the Jewish Sabbath, in this version of bagel history, the baking was done quickly after the sun went down.

However, the Sabbath story is questionable. Another tale, which traces the bagel's origin to a Polish king's defeat of the Turks, is only a legend.

Many believe a bagel is lucky because it is round. A circle is a "perfect" symbol because it does not have a beginning or an end; since it is also considered a symbol of life, the Jewish childbirth story may have some credibility.

## Artisan Craftsmanship

Ingredients are not the only important elements of a bagel. The baking process, which cannot be rushed, is also important. The prep work, mixing, proofing, textures, and temperatures must all be nurtured and balanced to create superior artisan bagels.

Artisan bread is handcrafted and made in small batches at a bakery rather than in a factory. The baker handles raw materials carefully, using his or her understanding of the ingredients' chemical makeup and their reactions in combination.

A large part of the artisan process goes beyond the technical aspects; it involves using one's hands, head, and heart in making the bagels. The baker uses his or her creativity to perfect the process and craft a wonderful product.

When people smell fresh bagels and experience their chewy crunchiness, their faces light up. Bagel lovers are everywhere, especially on Sunday mornings, Monday afternoons, Tuesday nights at snack time... you get the idea. There are no rules or restrictions. Bagels broke out of the breakfast-food-only category long ago. People now eat them day and night, at meals and in between.

People's love of bagels has become universal. Quite unexpectedly, I found myself right in the middle of this culinary trend.

## My Introduction to Bagels

I grew up in Bay City, Michigan, in the 1960s and 1970s. In that time and place, bagels were not common. I had eaten a few frozen bagels at friends' homes, but that was it. In my teenage mind, bagels were a totally Jewish thing because only my Jewish friends' families seemed to have them.

My older sister Darcie married into a Jewish family. Once a month, her father-in-law, whom we all called "Grandpa"

Levinson, would drive one hundred miles each way to Ann Arbor to buy fresh bagels. The bagels he brought back were the real deal and absolutely delicious.

I took an immediate liking to the bagels and to Grandpa Levinson for turning me into a bagel buff. Little did I know then that these round, doughy creations with holes in the middle would shape my entire life.

*Little did I know then that these round, doughy creations with holes in the middle would shape my entire life.*

Years later, I started to enjoy cream cheese and smoked salmon, but I immediately fell in love with the combination of cinnamon raisin bagels and butter with raspberry preserves.

Since then, I have had an affinity for bagels.

## Inside My Bakery

Someone comes in at 1:00 a.m. to turn on the equipment. That means lighting the fire in the oven, lighting the flame for the kettle, and switching on the other machinery. It takes about twenty minutes to get water boiling in the kettle and twenty-five to thirty minutes for the oven to reach the right temperature. Then the process of baking begins.

Employees move around with their shoulders back, chins up, non-skid work shoes on, hair pulled back, hats and aprons on, and hands washed. Everyone is ready. They prepare to bake by pulling racks of bagels out of the walk-in refrigerator, brewing coffee or tea for jolts of caffeine, and smelling the bagels as they begin to rise. As the shop and bagels heat, everyone warms up.

By 4:30 or 5:00 a.m., our delivery vehicles are loaded and the first "bake" hits the streets, going to wholesale customers for resale.

The rest of the day is filled with mini bakes—just enough to keep the retail baskets in our store fresh and full until the 10:00 p.m. closing. We carefully gauge these bakes based on how many customers come through the door or place orders via the Internet or the phone. Creating our artisan bagels, which take hands, head, and heart to master, is a study in balance.

# Chapter 2:
# ENTREPRENEUR BY NECESSITY

*Of course we build our castles in the air.*
*That's where they should be.*
*Then we have to build a foundation under them.*

—**HENRY DAVID THOREAU** (philosopher)

I start my workday at 4:00 a.m., so I normally get out of bed around 3:30 a.m. After being in the bakery business for years and years, early rising has become something I cherish, even though my initial reasons for getting up so early no longer really exist. Now my employees handle the early morning work.

I love the early morning's peace and quiet. I still go into the shop to hang out with the bakers some mornings. There's nothing like the smell of wet yeast boiling and fresh bread baking.

## Not Part of the Plan

If you had asked me when I was younger what I planned to accomplish in my life, I would have answered something having to do with gymnastics or the law. I would not have said, "Become an entrepreneur." Yet that entrepreneurial spirit turned out to be an integral part of my personality and my business life.

Being in the right business is much like feeling at home. It is like hitting middle C on a piano or tuning a string instrument to an A: it is when everything vibrates beautifully. I also compare it to the gymnast doing a split leap and feeling that second in the air when everything seems to stop in a perfect timeless moment.

I love losing myself in work—especially when it becomes a spiritual thing. I do not think that happens by magic; rather, it happens as a confluence of hard work, timing, and preparation.

*Being in the right business is much like feeling at home. It is like hitting middle C on a piano or tuning a string instrument to an A: it is when everything vibrates beautifully.*

What gets in my way most of the time, when the process does not work quite right, are fear and anxiety. I am caught in a never-ending effort to strike fear and anxiety from my lexicon, but I doubt they will ever be completely banished. In the meantime, I am satisfied with limiting my negative thinking to only occasional bouts of doubt.

## Getting Pregnant

While I was in law school, I seldom saw Razz, but when I did, our passion was intense. Our powerful physical attraction for each other is hard for me to recall now, but it was there.

When I finished my first grueling year of law school, I found out I was pregnant with Razz's child. While I had previously made it clear to him that I was not on birth control, he refused to wear condoms.

More than once I had asked what we would do if I got pregnant. "We'll get married," he said. Naïve me: I believed him. I love children and always imagined having a large family. I never imagined the man to whom I made love would lie to me.

Well, I got pregnant, and Razz did not want the child. What's more, he did not want anything to do with me. I felt betrayed and ashamed. I did not know which way to turn.

I had moved out of my house, which I shared with others, and was living with Razz in his apartment. Another student was renting my room at the house, so moving back was not an option.

I could not stand to be in the same place as Razz when he did not want our baby or me. So I took a bag of my clothes and went to stay at a youth hostel in downtown D.C. I put everything else I owned in the trunk of my '66 Chevy.

I felt totally alone and did not know what to do or where to turn. I knew I needed help, so I called my former boyfriend, who was seventeen years older than I was. He told me having an abortion was okay. However, I could not imagine terminating a pregnancy. I began looking at my alternatives.

I considered having the baby and giving it up for adoption— that way, he or she could be raised by two parents in a loving home. I deeply loved my baby, and I figured that Razz would always be remotely involved in my life if we had a child together. I decided it was best to have the baby and put it up for adoption.

Giving my child to someone else to raise seemed like one of the largest, most giving things I could do. Yet I knew Razz was adamantly opposed to adoption. I was scared of having to deal with his anger for the rest of my life.

Why I felt obliged to tell Razz about my decision is beyond me now, although communication has always been important to me. Razz went nuts about my plan to give the child up for adoption. I have never seen anyone that upset and angry; his reaction scared me. I still cared what he thought, too.

On the advice of my former boyfriend, I called my parents and discussed the situation with them. I was desperate. They listened and gave their support to whatever decision I reached.

I am sad to say that, in the end, I aborted my baby. It tore me apart, but I did it. I still live with thoughts of that child's identity.

Razz showed up at the abortion clinic, but I could not talk to him. Just looking at him made me nauseous. He took me back to my hostel and left me there. I remember lying in bed, all alone, cuddled up in a blanket and holding my belly. I could not believe where I was and what I had done.

After the abortion, I tried to study my law books. A couple of friends took notes for me in classes. However, I was a mess and grieving miserably. After several days, I reached out to one of the classmates who lived in my old house. I had to get out of the hostel. She agreed to let me sleep on a mattress in her room.

For two months, we slept one foot apart. It was a rough time. I survived on my classmate's kindness and energy. I was stressed, angry, and lonely, so I immersed myself in studying. I hated myself for being so stupid, yet I challenged myself to forgive Razz and to love more deeply. My sense of religion dictated that I come to a state of forgiveness and love.

## Razz Comes Around

It almost seemed as though Razz cared for me more after I aborted the child. Only much later did I realize that being the recipient of caring from another person does not mean much if you do not love yourself.

Despite the horrible experience of the abortion, or perhaps in part because of it, Razz and I moved in together again. This time, I kept renting a room that had opened up at my old house, just in case. After all, Razz and I did not have a great track record.

Soon, Razz's utilities were cut off, and he failed to pay rent. We ended up moving into my rented room after all. In hindsight, warnings should have been going off in my head about his lack of financial savvy and responsibility.

Instead, we planned to get married.

Although Razz and I intended to elope, our respective parents encouraged us to have at least a small ceremony and celebration with our families present. Razz had grown up, in part, at his grandparents' house on Martha's Vineyard, and his mother still lived there. He and I took a quick trip up to his family's place to check out every church on the island. First Congregational Church in West Tisbury was simple, bright, and airy, so we chose it.

## Wedding Blues

Razz and I got married in Tisbury Chapel on a perfectly beautiful July morning after I completed my second year studying law. I planned a Sunday morning ceremony to avoid the heavy drinking that would likely occur at an afternoon or evening wedding.

Our wedding looked pretty, but it was uncomfortable for me. The best part was that all my brothers and my sister came with their families. My sister and niece stood beside me, and each of my brothers had a special verse to read.

BAGEL WISDOM

**BEYOND THE BAGEL:** Georgetown Bagelry specializes in bagels; we make bagel sandwiches and plain and fancy varieties of bagels. We also make some complementary baked goods, like blueberry and cranberry muffins.

Though we use fruit to make the muffins, trust me: we will never make fruitcake. Never. Not Jamaican or any other kind.

When I walked down the aisle with my father, the church pews on the right— on Razz's side—were nearly full. We had agreed to have just family at the wedding, so I had not invited my friends (a fact I regretted later). Yet my new mother-in-law had invited many of her friends.

The left side of the church—my side— was empty except for the first two pews, which held my family.

After the simple ceremony, we had a champagne brunch at the Beach Plum Inn overlooking Menemsha Harbor. It was a charming place. Razz's mother had had a Jamaican wedding cake made in New York City and brought to the Vineyard. It looked beautiful—tiered and intricately decorated—but it was a fruitcake and tasted awful. There was so much brandy in it that people were gagging.

Darcie and I laughed so hard we cried. Neither of us could believe how Razz's family had made such a big deal about what turned out to be an awful cake.

After the reception, our entire group spent the day on South Beach. We swam, relaxed in the sun, read, and visited with each other. The guys drank beer. It was pleasant.

# Chapter 3:
# PASSION AND PROBLEMS

*Adversity has the effect of eliciting talents, which in
prosperous circumstances would have lain dormant.*

—**HORACE** (Roman poet)

## Basic Ingredients

Great bagels do not happen without passion. Bagels
have basic ingredients: flour, yeast, water, sugar,
and salt. However, the difference in the final results
is influenced in large part by the careful selection
and balance of those ingredients, plus the passion and spirit the
baker puts into the process.

Many variables go into the artisanal bagel process. I make
all the decisions about our bagels' numbers, look, feel, texture,
and taste.

People talk about New York bagels, surmising that New
York water makes the bagels better. Fresh water varies depending
upon where in the world you are, but in my experience, the key
to making a great bagel is regulating the water's temperature.

## How to build a bagel.
## Ingredients matter – a lot.

**Flour:** The quality of the flour we use makes a huge difference in the texture of each bagel. Flour is not the same year to year, unless you use a high-quality, unbleached, highly-processed, high-gluten, expensive flour milled from a select blend of hard red wheat.

Farmers harvest this wheat in a few different places in the U.S. The best manufacturers do not allow wide variations in the type of wheat used for this flour. There are lower-grade and lesser-processed flours, but we use the best—even when commodity prices fluctuate. My bagelry is a business, so of course price is important; however, how the flours blend is more important.

**Sugar:** We use light brown sugar in our bagels. We use it like simple sugar. We take cups of sugar, add water, and stir over a low heat until the mass turns to liquid.

**Salt:** We use regular, iodized, and granulated salt in the bagels. We use Kosher pretzel salt on four types of bagels: salt, garlic/salt, everything, and "happiness" (the latter are pumper-nickel bagels coated with hulled sesame seeds and a little bit of coarse pretzel salt).

**Yeast:** The wet yeast we use is delivered to us in cases of one-pound blocks. Visualize one pound of butter. That's the size of a pound of wet yeast.

**Water:** Our bagelry, where we make bagels, is several hours south of New York. Our tap water may be warmer in temperature than New York tap water. During hot weather, we add ice to cool our water before pouring it into the mixer.

## The Right Percentages

Our bagels have never been better than they are right now. Much of that has to do with the flour. It dawned on me recently that even though I have consistently ordered the same brand of flour for years, that does not mean the flour is grown in the same fields or milled in the same mill year after year.

To experiment, I asked for specs on a multitude of flours from different suppliers. I absorbed all the information, went with my gut, and made some changes. It was the absolute right move, and my intuition proved spot on.

Everyone working in the shop is happy because they all see the difference in the flour quality. My bakers display big, fat grins of amazement.

It is pretty cool to figure this stuff out. It is part science, part creativity.

## Dreams and Reality

*...And a glimpse into the future...*

The night of our honeymoon, Razz went to bed early and passed out. I could not believe it.

My brother-in-law, his girlfriend, and one of my girl-friends—the only friend I had invited to the wedding—went skinny-dipping in the country club pool where we were staying. I tried to wake Razz because I thought it would be good for us to join them.

However, Razz insisted I leave him alone. He had done enough and wanted to sleep. I bugged him but got nowhere. He was an occasional blackout drinker, but, at that point, I really did not have a clue what that meant.

With my husband passed out in bed, I joined the others and went skinny-dipping, which was just old-fashioned fun. When I was growing up in Bay City, whenever the weather was warm enough, we went skinny-dipping. It was a normal, fun thing for me to do.

While our group was in the pool, Razz woke up and came outside. He made a huge scene about how I was skinny-dipping with his brother, even though we were obviously swimming at opposite ends of the pool. Razz was terribly drunk. His words and actions were outrageous.

I got out of the pool and dressed before going back to our room. I felt as though my independence and unique, personal identity had disappeared.

I could not believe how drunk Razz was on our wedding night. I had never seen such anger; I felt as though I were with an absolutely crazy stranger. We yelled and screamed, slamming doors. We had a living battle of egos. Someone even called the police.

On my wedding night, I decided to leave. I slipped out and walked down to the beach. At that moment, I felt there was no way in the world I was going to stay married to this man. I knew my family would understand. Clearly, I had made a horrible mistake.

I sat on the beach, numb, trying to contemplate what to do next. I prayed.

Then Razz's brother joined me and talked me into not ending the marriage. I eventually went back to my room, slept, and woke up early the next day. I was very unhappy. Razz apparently remembered nothing about what had happened. I could not figure it out. I did not yet know much about blackouts and alcoholism.

I did not want to face my family, so I was relieved we were leaving the island that day. We had to get back to the bagel shop, and I had a summer internship arranged. Ironically, my job was to interview victims and defendants in domestic violence cases, one after another.

*I helped many people, but I did not know how to help myself. I needed help, but I did not know how to ask for it.*

I completely identified with the fear and terror of the women involved. They saw no way out and kept going back to abuse; it was familiar, and they hoped it would change. This was a tough job for me because I was in an abusive relationship myself.

I helped many people, but I did not know how to help myself. I needed help, but I did not know how to ask for it. It took me a long time to learn.

This time was the beginning of a big gap in my relationship with my parents and siblings. I did not want to tell them the truth about Razz, especially after having aborted a child and then going back and marrying this man, like that would fix something. I was not sure what was broken, other than my heart.

## Adding Insult to Injury

The beginning of my marriage was horrible.

My new mother-in-law came to visit soon after we were back in D.C. She stayed for five weeks. Her visit did not help.

## Over His Head

The bagel business was booming. Our bagels were the best in the entire city, and our largest wholesale account wanted to expand, bringing bagels into all their locations. To meet demand, we needed a production facility. The shop in Georgetown did not have the capacity to produce the number of bagels we needed.

Just before our marriage, Razz and I opened a factory in Landover, Maryland, quadrupling our production capabilities. After our marriage ceremony, I began my third year of law school. Razz had his hands full between the factory and the retail shop.

And what did I do? I immediately got pregnant again. Of course, this was unplanned. By that fall, I was a pregnant law student with a spouse who raised questions about every guy with whom I came in contact. It is no wonder I was stressed and unhappy. I did not realize it until later, but I was pregnant when we married. Unbelievable.

My law school class was 75 percent male, and my new husband had made it clear that he did not trust me around other men. This was another red flag. Already there were many, many red flags. And then another pregnancy!

Razz was struggling with the factory end of our business, and he was concerned about theft at the shop. He did not trust anyone there either. I could not concentrate in law school because of the turmoil in our relationship, and Razz really needed help.

My law professors and fellow classmates already thought I should go into business instead of the law. In addition, I was making a great deal of money selling sandwiches and bagels near the school. I decided to drop out of school and help with the business.

I loved bagels and was already interested in the business. While my decision was born out of necessity it held appeal for me as well.

## Drinking

Early in my relationship with Razz, I rarely drank any alcohol. I would have an occasional glass of wine, but Diet Coke and tea were my drinks of choice. I grew up without alcohol at home, and my previous boyfriend did not drink. I was naïve and ignorant about drinking and alcoholism. That was quickly going to change.

My marriage to Razz was horrible. There I was, pregnant. For the second time, I terminated a pregnancy because I did not want to bring a child into a fractured home. While this was a grueling decision, deep down I knew I could not go through with the pregnancy.

I did not discuss my decision with Razz until after the fact. After one abortion, it was not quite as emotionally difficult for me to have the second one. I wished I had used birth control, but I did not. I was paying the consequences of poor choices.

About a week later, I told Razz. We were out on our front stoop in the poor neighborhood in which we were living. He had disappeared the night before; perhaps I was trying to get even. Razz burst into an angry fit, pouring the beer in his hand over my head. I stood there in shock and cried. I was not crying over my child, but over my situation.

I gathered some of my clothes and left. With no plan about where to go, I called my former boyfriend and told him I was scared. He directed me to come to his house, where he made me talk through what had happened. It was difficult for me to talk, but nothing was easy in my life.

Like just about everyone else I knew, my former boyfriend had never approved of my relationship with Razz. He thought the sooner I ended it, the better off I would be. After a long conversation, I spent the night in his guest room and slept well. However, I did not accept his advice, deciding instead that I would face my problem and work through it. Actually, there were several problems. In my mind, I could not simply run away or leave my marriage.

I went home the next morning. The house was empty. I walked around aimlessly for a bit before going to work. Razz was at the factory in Maryland, so although we worked in the same business, we were at different locations.

That evening, I got home after Razz. He was already in the kitchen cooking up a culinary storm, drinking beer, and humming along to flute and piano music on the stereo. I was flabbergasted and relieved, although his aura of nonchalance did not convince me that we did not have big problems.

I tried to discuss the events of the previous night, but Razz seemed not to understand any of it. I refreshed his memory and we talked, but he did not give me an apology or show any realization of what had happened.

I was astonished and began to fear for my life. This experience was like the one I had the night we got married, after which he seemingly remembered nothing about what had happened by the pool.

I was becoming more and more enmeshed into the crazy life of an addict—and, no doubt, co-dependent.

We had many of these conversations throughout our marriage. These experiences are not even believable to me when I try to wrap my head around them. However, they were real, and alcoholic blackouts can be deadly.

We developed a pattern of having confrontations in the evening while he drank liquor until either blacking out or passing out. Incredibly, this became the norm. Although I was bewildered and scared, I figured there had to be a solution, and I tried my best to figure it out.

Razz was often apologetic. Yet, in standard fashion for a participant in an abusive relationship, I thought I was the problem. I fooled myself into thinking that if only I just worked harder, meditated longer, and loved him more, things would work out.

While I was busy making the best of a bad situation, a few months later (surprise, surprise!) I was pregnant again.

## A Seemingly Long Pregnancy

I worked every day all the way through what was my third pregnancy. I wanted this baby more than anything. Yet it was a complicated birth, and my baby, Lucien, and I nearly died in the process.

Lucien was born by Cesarean section after a long, intense labor. It was difficult for the anesthesiologists to give me an epidural because the contractions came so hard and so fast. Although the pain was horrible, the moment I held Lucien in my arms, I was happy.

The labor caused damage to my spine and nerves. The doctors said it would take months before I got any feeling back. It took one month before I could walk at all and nearly two months until I could go back to work.

When I was finally feeling better, I set up a nursery in my office at the shop and took Lucien with me every day. This child was the most precious thing on earth to me.

# Chapter 4:
# LOVE GONE AWRY

*Sail away from the safe harbor. Catch the trade winds in your sails. Explore. Dream. Discover.*

—**MARK TWAIN** (author)

## A Crazy Life

I left law school a month into my third year. Razz was struggling with the bagel business and it looked as if we would not have much financial security unless we were both involved in the company. He spent all his time at the factory in Maryland, neglecting the retail operation in D.C. Cash was flying out of the business. No one, certainly not me, knew where it was going.

Everything was a mess. Razz had moved all the good equipment to the factory. We were not even producing bagels at the shop; we were only selling bagels made in our factory. We shipped over boards of bagels from the factory, and we boiled and baked them in the retail shop.

I was determined to give my commitment to our marriage its best shot. Razz had made off-the-cuff remarks about the men I was around in law school. It did not register with me until much later that this jealousy was a reflection of Razz's own disloyalty and infidelity. At the time, I thought leaving law school would help us.

Thus, for these, and a few other reasons, I decided to help out in the business. Once I recovered from my long labor and emergency C-section, I started showing up at the shop every day with Lucien in tow.

## A Tiny House

Once both Razz and I were working, the bagel business started to flourish. We were able to pool enough money to buy a small row house between the Potomac River and the C&O Canal in Georgetown, within walking distance of the bagel shop.

Our house was a charming, little, 600-square-foot, three-floor townhouse with a little garden out back. We loved it. Historically, this house and several others like it were living quarters for the servants of the wealthy people who lived in mansions north of M Street. I was definitely a laborer and felt at home there, especially after learning the house's history.

Razz and I worked long hours and played music together. That was about it. Once a week, we went out to eat.

The bagel shop became a social gathering place on Saturday and Sunday mornings, frequented by the "who's who" in the neighborhood and occasional celebrities who visited town.

Our life had a rhythm. Every morning, Razz would leave at 3:30 a.m., sometimes earlier, and stop by the retail store before heading out to the Maryland factory. In those early years, he often worked eighteen-hour, labor-intensive days.

I have never, before or since, seen anyone need to do physical labor so much. It was almost as if he was afraid to slow down because he might have to face himself.

Razz was his own worst enemy, and I thought I could make a difference. I began building trusting relationships with everyone who worked for him. I did this in a very quiet, subservient sort of way.

When push came to shove, instead of continuing to argue with Razz, I would back off and let him dig himself deeper. I did this to keep peace in the family. I was also frightened, afraid he might take his anger out on me or on our child, and that one of us would get seriously hurt.

We had a few arguments in private over operational and financial issues. Early on, it was clear that Razz was in control and all would be done his way.

## The Situation Gets Worse

The ten bakers at our Maryland factory worked horribly long, hot, and physically demanding hours. They usually worked ten-hour days, 6 days a week. Razz's management model put him at the helm. He was completely dominating, completely in charge, and always telling everyone else what to do.

On a hot day in June, led by a part-time college student Razz had hired, the workers decided to go on strike. They calculated that production could not happen without them, so they simply walked out—without a union, without a list of demands other than more pay, and without notice.

When they walked out, Razz chased them. They ended up actually running away from him. As you can imagine, Razz was furious. He expected everyone to work as hard as he did and to obey his demands unconditionally. Afterward, Razz called to tell me what had happened; he said he was going to need help.

I hit the road immediately. The factory was about a 45-minute drive from the Georgetown shop, and I brought a couple bakers from the D.C. location to help out. As soon as I arrived, I went in back by the ovens to evaluate the situation and get a grip on what was required to meet the demands of the bake for that day. The next thing I knew, there was shouting out front. I rushed to see what was going on. Six huge Maryland police officers were handcuffing Razz, reading him his rights, and forcing him into a paddy wagon.

I stepped in front of two of the biggest policemen and asked what was going on. At first, they did not even acknowledge me. I was persistent and kindly but firmly told them that I was Razz's wife and I wanted to know what the hell was going on. They said I could call the precinct later, and someone there would fill me in.

It turned out that the bakers had filed a petition against Razz, and that was all the police needed to put a warrant out for his arrest.

## 24,000 Bagels a Day

It was only 10:00 a.m. There I was with my husband arrested and a huge mix that needed to be done. We needed the mix so 2,000 dozen bagels could be produced by 2:00 a.m. the next morning: 24,000 bagels.

I had a one-and-a-half year old at home, and, although I did not realize it at the time, I was pregnant again. I was dumbfounded. It seemed to me as though I had already been through enough emotional stuff for a lifetime, and here I was again—thrust back in the midst of more drama.

I had enough sense to excuse myself and step away from the few workers I had brought with me. I went into the factory office, sat down in Razz's chair, took a deep breath, became still, and began listening for direction. I prayed. By remaining still and breathing deeply, I could feel my own heartbeat. When I listened quietly, my heart told me what to do.

*By remaining still and breathing deeply, I could feel my own heartbeat. When I listened quietly, my heart told me what to do.*

This was not the only time I sought out quiet so the next right thing to do would come to me. I had done it before and would do it many times again. In balancing my thoughts and stilling my emotions, I find a plan of action becomes available to me, and I am able to move forward.

## Immediate Concerns

The first thing I did was call Razz's best friend, who is also a lawyer, so he could get a handle on Razz's whereabouts and situation. He promised to update me as soon as he got any information.

Next, I called one of the women from the Georgetown shop who was at my home, taking care of Lucien for me. When I asked, she agreed to stay for the duration until I could figure things out.

I closed the Georgetown shop early and brought the few workers capable of production out to the factory. However, they were not factory workers; they did not have the technique, speed, or skills we needed.

However, sometimes you have to work with what you have. Together, we figured out what we needed to do to make production happen. We just started doing everything we could. It was a marathon.

I used every coaching technique on the planet to get us through that day. We played a Bobby McFerrin song, "Don't Worry, Be Happy," over and over on the boom box. The music kept us going when we were exhausted. We could not afford to stop; it would have been impossible to finish.

Somehow, with sheer will and determination, we got those 24,000 bagels ready by 2:00 a.m.

## Epiphanies

When Razz went to jail, bam! I was instantly running the bagel show.

I knew I needed help. I called each of my four brothers to see if any of them could fly out, but of course they all had their own jobs and young families for which they were responsible.

Next I called my dad, who flew in from Midland, Michigan, on the first plane available. The next thing I knew, Dad was walking into the bagel factory. I have never been so happy to see anyone in my life.

Dad had been a supervisor at a Dow Chemical plant for thirty-five years. He ran a tight ship and was highly respected. I never saw anyone organize a place so fast in my life as he did our bagel factory. I learned a great deal from him during the few days he was there.

Dad observed our set-up and befriended the workers by asking them questions about their personal lives and their work. From them, he learned the changes that needed to be made to make the factory processes easier. That first evening, he evaluated the situation and wrote it all down on paper, making a list of changes that we needed to implement.

Once we went back to my tiny house in lower Georgetown, where Dad was going to sleep on the couch for a few days, we sat at the kitchen table and talked over some iced tea. I put my feet up and saw that they were horribly swollen.

I looked at him and said, "Dad, look at my feet. Please tell me I'm not pregnant again!"

His look spoke a thousand words. We both knew I was pregnant. I had tears in my eyes. Lucien was already tucked into bed. Despite our plan to get up very early, we went to sleep very late.

After he was released from jail, Razz went back to work. His workers dribbled back to work one at a time, day by day. The strike did not hold, in part because they failed to file a list of demands, and in part because they needed their jobs and did not think about the ramifications when they went on strike.

My father worked beside Razz for a few days, but I could tell I was his main concern. There were not any simple answers, especially with a baby on the way. I was scared and pregnant. I was living in a toxic situation without a roadmap for escape.

My father was strong and silent. I trusted him, so I tried to be the same.

## My Childhood

Growing up, it tore me apart that my Dad used his words so sparingly. I wanted to know what he was thinking and how he felt, but he did not talk to me much. I think he was afraid of giving the wrong advice or letting us see his soft side.

He was a man of few words, at least to me. Yet when he did speak, his words had the effect of hitting the bull's eye—they were spot on. Although he did not talk a lot, he sure thought a lot and he was a man of action, preferring to do things rather than talk about them.

As a little girl, I practiced the piano almost daily. My mother would try to get me to finish playing before Dad came home, so he could read the newspaper in peace. However, the truth was that I would finagle whatever I could to end up practicing when Dad got home.

I would wait until he was sitting in the big chair next to the piano, reading the paper, and then ask him if he minded if I played. I hated the idea of practicing, but once I sat down and started, I loved it. My dad *loved* this stupid little song called "Baby Elephant Walk." I can hear it in my head right now. He loved big band music, and this piece had that kind of a lilt.

It is not always enjoyable listening to kids learn and practice music, but I believe my father learned a lot about me from how I played the piano. Mom said she could tell how I was feeling by how I played my music. True.

I was Daddy's little girl.

My older sister, Darcie, and our dad had an entirely different relationship. He was pretty tough on her, but by the time I came along (eight years later), my parents were more laid-back.

I have two older brothers: Mike is six years older and Pat is four years older. I also have two younger brothers: Badger (who has my mother's maiden name as his given name) is five years younger and Bobby is eleven years younger. Darcie was twenty-one and getting married when Bobby was born.

While Dad always came through for me, I felt he was more interested in the boys because they had so much more in common. Dad coached their Little League teams, and they all played basketball and football. Of course, the dinner table conversation was sports talk. Mom would try to bring up world news, but such conversations usually ended up in fights over differing opinions.

I was a gymnast and very athletic, but the guys did not want to talk about full twists, split leaps, or dancing.

We went skiing almost every weekend throughout the winter. We would get up at 5:00 a.m., load the car with gear, pack food (because we could not afford to buy it and there were too many of us), and hit the road for the three-hour trip to Caberfae Peaks, in northern Michigan. We were there when the slopes opened, and we were often the last to leave.

I did not like to ski with my dad because he was not very daring. He loved to take me to the back slopes where we could ski the trails. He liked the roundabout way. I hated sitting on the chair lift with him in silence. He would give me advice on being careful or on how to ski, but I did not listen or respond. Maybe I was the silent one.

# Chapter 5:
# PICKING UP THE PIECES

*Jealousy in romance is like salt in food. A little can enhance the savor, but too much can spoil the pleasure and, under certain circumstances, can be life-threatening.*

—**MAYA ANGELOU** (author)

## Winning

**G**rowing up, Dad never let me win at anything. Whether we were playing cards, skiing, or playing catch or badminton in the backyard, I never won. I sure as hell tried, and it was frustrating, but it made me strong and determined to improve in whatever I was doing.

I learned that winning is not everything; instead, through participating, I increase the potential for living my life more fully. Witnessing someone else winning is often just as satisfying as winning yourself. It took me years to understand this principle, and it is now a part of how I handle business.

Creating a workplace where everyone shares ideas and voices their authenticity makes everyone a winner and establishes a win-win situation.

Nearly every time I walk into the bagel shop, customers compliment me on how well my employees treat them. In truth, I do not think of my employees as "employees," but rather as "partners." This shift of thinking makes for a better work environment.

I let my customers know that we spend plenty of times behind the scenes getting to know each other by sharing details about our lives and passions.

## Gymnastics

The summer before I went to tenth grade, I had a chance to move to Maryland where I would enter special gymnastics training with some of the top girls and coaches in the country. My parents gave me the go-ahead. I planned to live at a coach's house, go to a nearby school, ride my bike to the gym, and teach at the gym to help earn my keep.

Shortly before it was time to go, my parents sat me down and told me they had changed their minds. They had decided it was more important for me to live at home and be with the family than it was to train more thoroughly in gymnastics. I was devastated.

To soften the blow, my father bought me a set of uneven parallel bars and a balance beam that we put in our backyard. This was a big deal. The equipment was expensive, and I knew my folks could not really afford it.

I knew Dad hated to see my dreams melt, so he gave me the best help he could by learning to judge gymnastics, just as he had been there for my brothers in Little League.

Dad came through for me when it was important. Often, when he knew I was upset about something, or if he could catch me for a few minutes to sit down, he would ask me to have a cup of iced tea with him on the front porch.

He would say, "Come on; let's have a cup of tea." How many dads sit and have tea with their daughters? Mind did—often. We would sit on the top step of the front porch, drink our tea, and talk. I learned a lot about hunting and fishing from these talks.

I remember coming home some evenings after practice. Dad would be sitting on the front porch with several of my guy friends from school clustered around and talking with him. I think he talked more to them than he talked to me.

## Between a Rock and a Hard Place

After about a week, Dad left Washington, D.C., and life went on. It was horrible. My husband was obviously over his head in the business, and I was pregnant for the fourth time. I love children more than anything in the world, but it was a long winter.

The workers filed charges, and Razz went to court. One of the workers said Razz had beaten him. I knew only too well my husband's flashes of anger, so I asked Razz if it was true. He said no, but he had chased the workers, and he was so furious that had he caught them, he would have hurt them.

In the end, the charges did not hold.

After watching my father step in and institute processes and simple systems at the factory, it was obvious to me that Razz lacked the experience, knowledge, and desire to sustain quality bagel production, let alone to take the business to the next level.

Running a small business is very different from running a larger business.

About a month after his arrest, my husband did not come home one night. It was the middle of the week, so I called the factory to find out what was going on. I imagined a piece of equipment had broken down or there were extra orders to fill. It was unusual that Razz had not called to say he would be late. He always had explanations for everything.

I could not locate him, and none of the employees knew his whereabouts. If they did know, they did not want to tell me. I called the Maryland police, but they had nothing to tell me.

Finally, I called Razz's best friend. He tracked Razz down and found out he had been picked up for soliciting a prostitute in D.C.; Razz was in jail. I was devastated.

*In my heart, I promised myself that I would raise my boys to be the opposite of their father. I promised myself to lead them in conscience and consciousness.*

I tried to separate myself from Razz's behavior, but it was not easy. I could not imagine why he would do something like this when I was his partner and spouse—and I thought I was good at it. After all, I was always forgiving him.

What I did not see at the time was that I was enabling Razz's behavior.

After his lawyer bailed him out, Razz came home with a poor excuse, swearing there had been no sexual contact. According to him, oral sex did not count. I forced myself to half-believe him.

At the time, I convinced myself the only thing that really mattered to me was living the best way I could. That meant spending one-on-one time with Lucien and preparing for the birth of my next son.

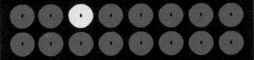

**BAGEL WISDOM**

**BABY STEPS:** When my kids were little, I told them I was from Mars. I did not think they would really believe me, but they did and they were fascinated. That lasted for a pretty long time.

I told them I had landed in a little bubble, and my parents had found me in Great-Grandma Badger's cornfield when they were taking a shortcut to plant pine trees on the back forty acres.

The kids asked me why I had them do goofy things like strap sponges with rubber bands around their feet so they could help me wash the kitchen floor. They would ask where I learned to do it, and I would say, "Oh, that's how we did it on Mars."

We also made sleds out of boxes and pizza pans. I carried a squirt gun in my pocket sometimes, just to surprise them.

We did not have much in terms of physical possessions, but we sure had lots of fun.

In my heart, I promised myself that I would raise my boys to be the opposite of their father. I promised myself to lead them in conscience and consciousness.

While all this drama was revolving around me, I went to church every Sunday; there, I received strong metaphysical support. That was the only avenue open to me, for I did not dare share my marital difficulties with anyone.

I prayed to be led in a positive direction. How that would unfold was a huge mystery to me, but I intended to live a respectable life and honor my creator by being the best possible version of myself. I knew I had to define what that meant for me.

It was a slow yet steady process. While I was undergoing it, I observed other people and their relationships. I spent each day doing the best I could.

It was an intense time; I had a small child and no extended family nearby. I had no one with whom I felt I could talk honestly.

## Day by Day

I did not have a big picture of where my life was going, or where the craziness would lead, but I tried to love more every day—whatever that meant. Somehow, I found meaning in waking up and giving each day my best shot.

Razz left home at various early morning hours ranging from 1:00 to 4:30 a.m. This was 365 days a year. Whenever he left, I quickly got up afterwards. Typically, I had a few hours before the kids woke up.

In those early hours, I read every spiritual book I could get my hands on, and I did the housework. I also wrote journal entries and poetry, but I always threw my writing out because I did not want Razz to find it. I was afraid that some of my writing would trigger his craziness, and things had grown more harmonious. Unfortunately, I did not know drugs were fueling Razz's sleeping habits and manic behavior.

Still, I found newness in each day, and I was learning more about myself. We lived in an appealing, urban place—Georgetown, with several universities nearby and diverse people filtering through.

## Spirituality

When things were really awful and I felt overwhelmed, I would ask myself, "What would God do?" If this did not spark an answer, I would turn to the wind and the soft breeze. Knowing the pure air was there to support me gave me hope.

As a yoga practitioner would, I find inspiration in each breath I take, especially when life is spiraling downhill. I feel the answers in my heart. Often, before the answers come, I take a long walk, play the piano, or go cycling. Somehow, these activities shift the paradigm and slow my brain, stopping it from feeding my doubts and fears. After a shift, I hear from my heart.

*One thing that cannot be taught is the passion that goes into the process of baking and creating great bagels.*

## Studying the Business

During this difficult period, I put in as much time as possible in the bagel shop, trying to learn everything. I waited on customers and worked side by side with everyone, from the front to the back of the operation.

I had always spent as much time as possible shadowing Razz at the factory while he created food. There was no question that he had the special touch, feel, and intelligence for baking. I wanted to learn as much as possible, so if anything happened to him, I could continue to use the business as a source of income and a way to provide for the children.

One thing that cannot be taught is the passion that goes into the process of baking and creating great bagels. The desire to make the best bagel possible is crucial. This desire becomes part of the pleasure and, ultimately, part of the final product.

At that point in my life, because I was so focused on loving the children and giving them the gifts and tools they needed to live a rich, full life, I tried to picture the worst-case scenario. Even then, I did not imagine how difficult things would get.

## A Particularly Bad Night

It had been a long day. As usual, we had all gotten up early: Razz at 4:30 a.m., me a half-hour later. I rose then so I could do as much around the house as I could before getting the kids up. This included laundry, cleaning, making lists, and preparing for the kids' music lessons.

I kept the kids on an early schedule, too; otherwise, they would make too much noise in the evenings when their dad was sleeping. Razz typically crashed in front of the TV by 8:00 p.m. Over the years, I had started urging him to watch TV from bed, so he would not have to get up and move or sleep all night in a chair.

On this particular day, Razz came home late in the evening, long after the kids were in bed. I had no idea where he had been, and I had stayed up worrying and drinking vodka. For a few years, I had been turning to vodka—straight up—to ease my pain.

I knew Razz was not working late because I had called the work locations. (This was before cell phones gave us a way to reach people wherever they might be.)

More and more, I had been finding traces of other women on Razz's clothing. I found lipstick that was not my color on the collar of his shirt and on his underwear; I saw long blonde hair clinging to his jacket or pants. I did all the laundry, and it was clear that he was seeing other women.

Frequently, I considered separating or divorcing because of Razz's indiscretions, but I could not stand the idea of not having full custody of the kids. I could not bear the idea of my kids going back and forth between us, or the thought of their father being with them and no one else to protect them. At this point, I clearly understood the danger he posed.

I could not imagine how to get free.

Sometimes, I would ask him about the lipstick or the blonde hair or the remnants of strange perfume. If I pursued such a conversation, it would turn into a full-blown argument. I had started drinking more, which did not help my judgment concerning confrontations. I pushed every button and pulled every trigger while trying to get Razz to be honest.

When confronted, Razz would flip the conversation around and bring up men with whom I had contact in passing: fathers at violin group classes, soccer dads on the sidelines at games, or fathers at school activities. He would insinuate that I was flirting. If I was sober, I could handle such a conversation. After all, I could not imagine looking at other men in a sexually provocative way.

On this particular night, I did not shut up. The kids were two floors up, sleeping. Razz grabbed my neck with both hands and told me to shut up. He began to strangle me. I could not breathe. At one point, he loosened his grip slightly, and I taunted him, "Go ahead. Kill me." I felt as if I had nothing left. I could feel my oxygen cutting off, and I heard him say how much he hated me.

My mind went dark, and I felt warmth as I thought of my children. God was telling me there was hope. I let go of all thought as Razz threw me to the floor and stormed upstairs. I could not breathe, and I could not talk. Somehow, while I was on the brink of death, life seeped back and I gasped for air. Blood came back into my head. I could see again, and I wept while holding my throat.

*My mind went dark, and I felt warmth as I thought of my children. God was telling me there was hope.*

I crept to the kitchen and tried to drink water, but it would barely go down. I could tell I had sustained real damage to my throat. I was afraid to make any noise; I was afraid for my life. I crawled back to the living room and lay down on the couch.

Crying, I managed to calm myself down enough to sleep. After all, I had to be able to take care of the children early in the morning.

# Chapter 6:
# UN-HOLY MESS

*Today you are You, that is truer than true.*
*There is no one alive who is Youer than You.*

—DR. SEUSS (author)

## The Next Day

When I finally woke up, Razz was gone, and the children were not yet awake. I stood in front of the mirror in the little bathroom next to the kitchen on the lower floor. I looked deep into my own eyes, trying to find where I was. Nothing seemed real. My neck was bruised, and I could not talk, only whisper. I knew my neck and throat were seriously damaged.

On top of the physical harm, I was horribly ashamed that my life had deteriorated so badly.

After I got the kids off to school, I drove to a quiet park and sat in my car. I cried and cried, trying to understand my situation. There were no answers. I did not know how to escape, and I did not even know where to go for help. I was too ashamed to talk to anyone—I did not want anyone to know about the fear I felt every day. I was embarrassed for having made horrendous life choices.

Ironically, in law school I had spent time working with battered women. Now I was a battered woman myself. I was amazed by how it had crept up on me; yet, in hindsight, I understand alcohol and violence are powerful factors that can be hard to escape.

From my law school experience, I knew it was always smart for battered women to take pictures and have records of the abuse. I was unable to talk above a whisper, so I realized I needed to go to a doctor. I found a throat specialist and went to see him the next day.

The throat doctor was concerned about me. He took photos and x-rays. He said my voice box was very damaged and I could have been killed. He asked me if I was safe, speaking very carefully and clearly as I held back tears. Frankly, I did not know what I was, but I assured the doctor I would be okay. All I could focus on was my need to take care of the children.

The doctor repeatedly asked me to call him if I needed help; he gave me his number and several other numbers. This helped me emotionally because someone now knew about my dangerous situation and cared. I was still too ashamed to talk to anyone with whom I was close. The truth of the matter was that as my marriage became worse, I had become isolated. I got better and better about denying the ugly reality of my marriage. I had become a great enabler.

As usual, my husband did not remember what happened. He thought I had laryngitis. It took years for me to understand alcoholic blackouts. I had never even heard of a blackout prior to knowing Razz. He would have outrageous outbursts and behave extremely, bordering on acting as though he had bipolar disorder.

After a night's sleep, it was as if nothing happened, and he was back to his old charismatic self.

The problem was that I did not black out, so I remembered everything.

## Pivotal Moment

It was a wet spring day in Washington. I remember the sad wetness of the day and the smell of spring because it was loaded with the scent from cherry blossoms and azaleas.

After working at the bagel shop, I was relaxing at home and getting ready to go into "mom" mode. The kids would be back from school in an hour, and I was looking forward to the shift from working to being with Lucien, Badger, and Retha.

The mail plopped through the mail slot in the front door and hit the floor with a thud. The noise sliced through the peaceful silence. While I did not know it then, after that moment my life would never be the same.

I walked toward the door, as if in slow motion, and bent to pick up the mail. Among the bills and advertisements was a letter from a Maryland court addressed to my husband. I opened it, as I did all the mail. The letter advised Razz that he was delinquent in child support payments.

This is silly, I thought. *Razz does not owe me child support.* Though I often thought of divorce, I had never pursued it, for I feared losing full custody of my children more than anything else.

After I read the letter several times, it became clear that my husband had a child I knew nothing about. I felt faint and collapsed on the floor. I tried to breathe and clear my mind. As I lay on the dining room floor, I knew I needed help.

All kinds of thoughts raced through my mind. Foremost was the fact that the kids would be home in a few minutes. I realized I had to start being totally honest with myself from then on.

## A Strong Dose of Reality

The chatter in my head was like a kindergarten class of five-year-olds wearing tap shoes and dancing on my brain. I felt a desperate need for answers. My head pulsated with fear, anxiety, and pain. Each time I tried to make sense of the letter, it blurred and looked incoherent to me. I began to weep on the inside and shake on the outside.

This had to be a mistake, because the letter was not talking about one of my children. It stated that my husband had a two-year-old daughter by another woman—both of whom I knew nothing about.

Talk about freaking out. I freaked out big time. With my children about to walk through the door, I wondered how I would feel in their shoes. More importantly, I wondered how they would feel in their shoes twenty years from now, depending on how I communicated with them. Those 15 minutes felt like so many hours.

## No Going Back

The letter was opened. That was not unusual. I opened my husband's mail since he rarely opened it himself. Before I started reading his mail, the utilities for both the bagel shop and our home were cut off.

Razz would make elaborate, arguably interesting excuses for why these things happened—why the store was closed, a ceiling beam fell, or the roof leaked through to the kitchen—but the truth was that he did not pay attention to paperwork, pay his bills, or follow through on much of anything.

If Razz could not keep track of something in his head, it did not get tracked. Inebriated brains do this. His fines doubled; the car got impounded several times because he failed to pay parking tickets. Of course, these repercussions made life difficult, especially for me and the kids.

On that wet spring day, I wished I had not opened this particular piece of mail.

I read and reread the words on the page because I was sure they could not be right. I kept thinking it had to be a mistake. I blinked my eyes, hoping my vision would clear and I would just be staring at a letter from the IRS or something. At that moment, the IRS was looking really good. Yet all the blinking in the world would not change what was written on that paper.

## Phone Calls

It took every ounce of energy for me to remain calm when I called Razz. He did not deny the child. He was in New York City visiting his mother, who was ill. He said he would come home immediately. I told him not to come.

Whenever I do not know what to do next, I try to breathe deeply, be still, and listen to my heart. That might sound simple, but it is not. For me, breath is inspiration. As I inhale and exhale, each breath of air helps reshape my thinking. I learned to do this when I was pursuing athletics, and it has saved me on more than one occasion. Practicing this breathing technique has made shifting my consciousness much easier.

On that day, even my breathing technique was barely helping. The little tap-dancing committee in my head was going crazy, and I just wanted the clatter to quiet down. I lay on the dining room floor, looking up at the bottom of the beat-up, wooden dining-room table, and kept thinking, "This is not real." The table's underside, with all its stains and nicks, looked as messy as I felt. Later, I learned this was a panic attack, but at the time I did not know what was going on.

I collapsed further into myself and had a weird out-of-body experience. Lying there, I felt the need to call my mother. I picked up the phone, which felt like a fifty-pound weight, and dialed. I was embarrassed and next to speechless. I was crying and felt like I could not breathe. The only thing I remember is her saying, "Honey, listen to your heart and do the next right thing for you." I felt like I was dying. In truth, my life as I knew it was ending.

## Clues

In hindsight, I remember wondering why Razz was acting strangely over the few years before that letter fell through our mail slot. He was exercising more, drinking more, and opening another business. Everything about him screamed for more, more, and more; yet there was definitely an emotional distance between us.

Here was the culmination of years of deception. He was living a second life that I knew nothing about. Perhaps I had chosen not to know because it seemed easier in our already extremely difficult relationship.

There had been numerous red flags, but nothing this life-altering.

That day, as the kids came home from school, I desperately tried to pull myself together. I realized that eventually the kids were going to know what had happened, so I might as well tell them immediately. I imagined myself in their shoes. I would want to know if I had a half-sister, despite the initial pain. Equally importantly, I thought they should know why I was an emotional mess.

Down the road, I knew they would appreciate my honesty. We would mend together.

When they came home from school, we sat around the dining room table, and I told them the truth as I knew it. I stuck to what was written on the court document. I saw the kids' reactions and realized this was not enough. We all needed more information.

Explaining the situation to my children was difficult, but I needed them to know I would always be honest with them, even through tough times. At least they would not think I was going crazy for no reason.

The next day, after a serious bout of drinking and crying all night, I collapsed again. I was attempting to take care of the children, run the house, and keep tabs on the three business locations Razz and I had at the time: two bagel shops and a pizza shop.

I focused on keeping the kids in their routines, fed, and loved. I was concerned about their reactions to the shocking information. Meanwhile, I thought I was having a heart attack.

Razz returned from New York and circled the house in his car, obviously contemplating the situation. The kids had left for school, and I had an awful hangover. I was scared to see him. The horrible aspects of our marriage were running like tickertape through my head.

When he finally came in, nothing he said made any sense.

Razz told me the mother of his other child was a prostitute whom he had known for years, even before he had known me. She was a former heroin addict, but she was supposedly okay now. The point he tried but failed to make was that this other woman was not a threat to me.

At this point, I had no reason to believe him. I asked him to leave for a few days, so I could have time to think. He plopped himself on the couch and said he was not leaving.

"Either you leave, or I am leaving with all three kids," I said. I was dead serious. Thank God he left.

## Asking for Help

I cried and cried; I could not breathe. I went to the emergency room at the nearest hospital, which was about half a mile from our house. I could barely drive myself there. I was shaking and had the worst headache of my life. I thought I was having a heart attack and was going to die.

The hospital personnel took my condition seriously. The doctors and nurses patiently encouraged me to find words to express the trauma. I was so miserable that I just wanted to stay in the hospital forever or die. The only things keeping me functioning at all were the kids.

The hospital sent a psychiatrist to talk with me. She said there were three things I needed to do to survive and work through my problems: eat three meals a day, exercise, and rest.

She made me understand that I could not take care of anyone else, including my kids, until I took care of myself. She also made it clear that I needed to know who I was, where I was going, and what I wanted to do. I needed to do "Mary" things like walking, keeping a journal, and playing the piano to figure that out.

*She also made it clear that I needed to know who I was, where I was going, and what I wanted to do.*

It sounds simple, yet doing those things was unbelievably challenging. I trusted her experience and did not question her advice.

Before I was released that day, the psychiatrist insisted I be tested for every sexually transmitted disease imaginable. Waiting for the results would create weeks of added anxiety, yet I was taking a smart step toward taking care of myself.

The psychiatrist also gave me a week's worth of sedatives to help me relax. I took them.

Thankfully, mercifully, when the results of the tests came back, I learned I had not contracted any diseases. I said more than one prayer of thanks when I learned this good news.

# Chapter 7:
# RUNNING AROUND ROADBLOCKS

*If you run into a wall, do not turn around and give up. Figure out how to climb it, go through it, or work around it.*

—**MICHAEL JORDAN** (athlete)

I am good at making bagels; I am great at making mistakes. Mistakes create an opportunity for growth, but they are often painful ways of getting to that growth.

## Facing Reality

I forced myself to face the fact that my marriage was a mistake. I needed to know exactly what I was up against, so I decided to hire a private detective. I had to stop living a lie.

The private eye I hired was a former Marine who looked like the TV detective Kojak. He quickly provided me with photos of my husband's other daughter and her mother.

I took a look at the photos and then took a serious look at myself. I immediately stopped drinking alcohol. It was not easy, because I was in so much emotional pain, but I knew it was necessary. I continued attempting to keep things normal for the kids, but there was nothing normal about our situation.

I went to the other woman's house, where she lived with Razz's daughter. I sat outside for a long time. I prayed. I tried breathing. Finally I walked up and knocked on the door. I was not calm, merely numb.

## The Other Woman

She opened the door. I smiled and calmly introduced myself as Razz's wife. His two-year-old daughter ran by and waved at me. The little girl was beautiful.

I said, "We don't need genetic testing for this small one, do we?" The child looked just like Razz.

The woman invited me in. We sat on opposite ends of the couch and talked while the little girl, who had changed my life, went back and forth between us.

The woman was soft-spoken and nervous. I found out she was in recovery from alcohol and drugs, including heroin. Despite being eight years younger than me, she looked eight years older. In addition to the obvious toll from substance abuse, I found her appearance was creepy because we resembled one other.

I felt sorry for her. She kept her head tilted down, apparently embarrassed that her teeth were rotten and missing. Her hands were limp from needles being poked in her veins. She had sad eyes, too, but they looked happy whenever she spoke about the little girl.

Eventually, I asked about her relationship with Razz. She told me that he came over one afternoon after the little girl was born and asked if she was his. At that point, there was no doubt in my mind that my marriage was over. Just the day before, Razz had lied to me when he said he had never seen his other daughter.

The woman said Razz was kind to her. She repeated this several times. Apparently, she had had rough experiences with men and did not see beyond Razz's "kindness." Given the woman's missing teeth and general decay, I could not fathom what Razz was thinking.

The little girl sat on my lap, and I played with her. She was adorable. I knew that none of this was her fault.

I left more confused than when I had arrived.

## Razz's History with Prostitutes

Early in our marriage, I knew my husband was seeing prostitutes. We worked together and spent more time together than most couples did; yet, every once in a while, he ran out on an odd errand as soon as I arrived at the bagel shop.

Razz's errands typically took a couple hours. Supposedly, he went either to The Home Depot or to pick up something he forgot to order from a supplier. Typically, Razz would be covered in flour and the smell of sweat and bagels. He always had a legitimate-sounding excuse, like wanting to fix the plumbing.

Over the years, I had fleeting suspicions that he might be seeing other women or even prostitutes. Then, one afternoon, I found our family video camera on a counter near the laundry room. At first, I thought the kids had been playing with it.

Then I noticed oil smeared on the camera, which I thought was really odd. I found a trail of oily fingerprints leading into

Razz's basement workroom. After the trail suddenly ended, I started looking all around. Eventually, I found photos and little reels of video clips hidden above the heat duct. The photos and videos were of Razz having sexual acts with different young women. They looked about high-school age, but it was hard to tell.

My kids were still in school, and I knew Razz was probably on his way home. I quickly watched as many of the videos as possible. It was horrible. There was a great deal of oral sex. Frequently, he covered a girl's head with a towel so he would not see her face. The girls seemed drugged. I could not believe it. This was all filmed inside our home.

I knew this was evidence that could be used in a divorce. I hid the film and photos, anticipating the confrontation and craziness that would follow a conversation about them.

Razz came home before the kids did. I immediately asked him to explain. At first, he tried to deny my accusations, but the photos were undeniable. I did not know what to do. I knew I needed space to think, so I asked him to leave. He left for a few days while I maintained a normal routine with the kids.

I felt very much alone. As usual, I walked to work through the woods and along the canal, but there was no answer in the breeze.

*I realized what a huge mistake I had made by isolating myself and not forming a network of people with whom I could talk.*

I realized what a huge mistake I had made by isolating myself and not forming a network of people with whom I could talk.

A few days went by. Razz assured me he would never do any of this again. I did not believe him, but, unfortunately, I decided to forgive him again and let him come home.

**BAGEL WISDOM**

**CREATING A SUCCESSFUL BUSINESS:**

The bagel business gives me a place to experiment and practice what is meaningful to me. It is my playing field, and I have learned to play well.

It helps that I love to win.

## Finally, Divorce

I finally learned that some things cannot be figured out; in those cases, the only solution is to separate from the craziness. In my mind, I nicknamed Razz the "crazy-maker."

It took several more months, but I managed to extricate myself from Razz by obtaining a legal separation. After the proper amount of time, we divorced.

I got full custody of the children and the bagel business. Razz got the pizza business he had started somewhere along the line.

Our relationship is relatively amicable now, which is good for the children.

## Trial and Error

When I took over the business, the company had two different sales tax numbers. I did not know which was which, and I saw that they were being used interchangeably. That was a big mistake. I was so busy and had so much on my plate that it took me a while to notice. One was apparently for the factory and the other was for the shop. I have no idea why there was more than one in the first place.

I hired various tax pros who were supposed to help with the tax mess. After spending a fortune for their expertise, I ended up simply figuring it out for myself. You have to pay your taxes. How complicated is that?

Once I realized what had happened with the sales tax numbers, I called the person in the State of Maryland who handles sales tax and explained the situation, asking for help from someone immediately associated with the issue. I stopped thinking about the problem and stopped deferring to supposed experts. Instead, I took action and asked for help. In this way, I found a solution.

## Learning the Hard Way

I made the mistake of signing contracts with two linen services at the same time. One had less expensive aprons and toilet paper; the other had a great rug service.

I did not want to fool around with the salespeople, so I did not take the time to thoroughly analyze what each had to offer. I just wanted the stuff, so I rushed through signing the contracts. We ended up overspending for no reason and receiving more products than we needed.

I decided to simplify things and deal with the consequences of not honoring one of the contracts. I told my apron guy his prices were too high and I could not afford to continue paying him. He was irate, and we had a heated conversation.

Afterwards, I felt I could have handled it better. I waited ten minutes to catch my breath, calm down, and think before I called back to apologize for being so harsh. However, I held firmly to my decision.

He also apologized and offered to give me unimaginably low rates on everything. I ended up cancelling the other contract and giving all my business to his company.

Through this experience, I learned not to act on a whim or to sign two contracts for virtually the same products. I explained to my team what had happened, thus encouraging them not to waste time hiding mistakes.

# Chapter 8:
# COVERED IN DOUGH

*Stay hungry, stay foolish.*

—**STEVE JOBS** (Apple co-founder)

## Meeting Jonathan

After my divorce, the last thing on my mind was a man. Several of my friends said, "We need to fix her up with someone."

I just wanted to be left alone. One friend kept talking about fixing me up over and over. I wanted to shut her up, so I finally agreed to meet a man she thought would be good for me.

I met Jonathan at Starbucks. I did not do any research ahead of time—not on Facebook, Google, or LinkedIn. I just went.

Meeting Jonathan was like being at a job interview, for he kept asking me questions. I thought to myself, "He doesn't realize that there's more to me than the answers to these questions, which seem superficial." It was annoying but kind of sweet, and it took almost exactly an hour, as if he were timing it.

It turned out he had been out with a lot of women and did not want to waste time. He told me he did not introduce anyone to his kids. On the surface, it certainly did not sound as though he was interested in a serious relationship.

After an hour, he stood up and said nervously, "I guess we don't have anything more to talk about."

I replied, "I guess not."

As we were going our separate ways, I turned around and saw that he was standing there checking me out.

One thing I liked about Jonathan right away was the expressiveness of his large hands. He has a wonderfully warm side that he rarely shares with other people until he gets to know them, and I only learned that later.

My friends were dying to know how the date had gone. I told them I thought Jonathan was rude and cheap. After all, he had not even offered to pay for my tea at Starbucks. The truth is that I was nervous and did not give him a chance to pay. I told my friends that Jonathan was not considerate just to get them to back off and stop pressuring me. He had actually arrived at Starbucks early and picked out the best table by the fireplace.

About two weeks later, I had tickets for a violin concert at the Kennedy Center. Despite his questioning me at our "interview" session, I knew Jonathan was tall and attractive and my friends seemed to like him. Although he had not called after the Starbucks episode, I called him to ask if he would like to join me at the concert.

"Absolutely," he answered without hesitation.

Then he sent me a list of relationship requirements via e-mail. I thought, "Oh, my God, what planet is this man from?"

This was wonderful—a man who knew what he wanted.

On his list were complete, total honesty and integrity. These were obviously good qualities. Having everything on the table was a great way to start a relationship. Jonathan does not mess around.

When we went to the Kennedy Center, Jonathan walked through the halls like he owned the place. He moved fast, like he does when he plays basketball; everything with him is big and fast. He also loves to be seated in front.

> *This was wonderful—a man who knew what he wanted. On his list were complete, total honesty and integrity.*

That night, Pinchas Zukerman was conducting and playing violin with a Canadian orchestra. We enjoyed the concert and enjoyed being with each other.

I found out that Jonathan was the ultimate camp counselor, always getting involved in his daughters' activities—like me with my children. I learned a little about his businesses and found that he loves to read, as do I. We did not get off to the best start, but our second date went much better.

Sitting next to each other in the concert hall, we wanted to touch one another, but we did not. We only talked about it later. We drove to a restaurant after the concert, repeatedly missing the correct street because we were so engrossed in one another.

## Zen and the Art of Making Bagels

Most customers have their favorites: poppy seed, sesame seed, cinnamon raisin, plain, pumpernickel, or garlic.

Then there are those who ask for "everything" bagels. Perhaps they like the combined tastes. Perhaps they want to experience everything in life. Or perhaps they dislike making decisions. There is a great deal of psychology that goes into choosing one's bagel.

And there is a myriad of toppings to choose from: butter, cream cheese, lox, peanut butter, pastrami, and so much more. Georgetown Bagelry supplies nurturing food and leaves the analysis to others, though after more than thirty years in this business, we have probably seen it all.

Mostly, choices are predictable. Yet we get surprised sometimes, especially by little kids who are experiencing bagels for the first time.

Traditionally, everything bagels (abbreviated as "ET" in the shop's vernacular), are plain bagels sprinkled with sesame, poppy, garlic, onion, and a little pretzel salt. We deleted caraway seeds (which are typically used in rye bread and are fruits, not seeds) years ago because they tended to get knocked off by the time the bagels were baked. Back then, if you were really lucky, you might have ended up with one or two caraway seeds still left on your ET bagel.

The same thing tends to happen with chopped onions—they fall off. However, we still put onions in our ET mix.

Complaints of one seed or another missing are common. Some bagel bakeries do not put all the seeds on their ET bagels because the price of commodities is high. Chopped onions are expensive for a forty-pound bag. Sesame seeds are pricey for a fifty-pound bag. These costs add up, but these items certainly help make our bagels special.

In our case, nothing is automated, so seeds on ETs vary ever so slightly, especially since different artisan bakers prepare them by hand each day.

Even the same baker will create slight variations from bake to bake. The human element adds distinct quality to our final products.

At Georgetown Bagelry, we put seeds on both sides of our bagels, even though doing so is more expensive. We sprinkle the burlap boards in the trough before placing the raw bagels on them. After preparing the long rectangular boards, we place bagels upside down on the boards. We sprinkle the bagel bottoms with the same varieties of seeds we use for the tops.

Next, we slide the boards onto the rotating stone shelves in the oven. Each row of bagels rotates until the bottoms are baked the perfect amount. We flip each board and bake the tops until they are golden brown.

Once they are baked on both sides, we lift the bagels out of the oven with a large flat paddle called a *peel*. In a practiced motion, the baker shifts the bagels from the peel into stainless steel wire baskets.

Since we put seeds on both sides, our bagels come out as if they have two tops—a fact our customers simply love.

## Special Stone

I have a "life purpose" stone from a beach on Lake Michigan. I almost always have this special talisman with me; that beach is the place I go to in my mind when I want to think.

The stone in my pocket comes in handy when I need to remember why I am doing what I am doing. Sometimes I hold it and affirm myself and my work with the mantra, "I am living an inspired life with an open heart, mind, and soul; this life is expressed through honesty and unconditional love and joy, by daily writing and action, in an easy and relaxed manner, and in a healthy and positive way for the highest good of all." I have recently added what I believe to be a cosmic insurance policy: "for this or something better." Often, I dream too small, so I am trying to open my thinking to ideas beyond my immediate imagination.

*Often, I dream too small, so I am trying to open my thinking to ideas beyond my immediate imagination.*

I found the stone one day when I was in Michigan walking along a dirt road. My younger brother Bobby had told me about a special beach at the end of Dead Stream Road. It is a little-known part of Sleeping Bear Dunes National Lakeshore on Lake Michigan. It is remote, peaceful, and spectacular in its pristine beauty.

The gorgeous, isolated beach represents home to me. You can smell the fresh water, so different from salt water, and the clear northern air and pine trees add to the place's unique nature. The beach is surrounded by tall grass and it is deserted, so you can sunbathe nude without getting caught.

Dead Stream Beach is where I found my small, smooth, black stone. I always have it with me. Sometimes I give it to someone who needs karma more than I do. Then, the next time I am on my hidden beach, I replace it.

BAGEL WISDOM

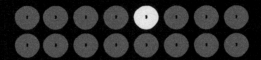

**BAGEL CODE**
**(like Morse code, only better):**

*pl* = plain

*ses* = sesame

*pop* = poppy seed

*ET* = everything

*ww* = whole wheat

*cinn/rais* = cinnamon raisin

*pump* = pumpernickel

*cran* = cranberry

*bb* = blueberry

*gran* = granola

*wwET* = whole wheat everything

*gar* = garlic

*salt* = salt

*on* = onion

*wwSes* = whole wheat sesame

*b&w* = black (pumpernickel) and white (plain)

*oat/rais* = oatmeal raisin

*gar/salt* = garlic salt

*minis* = mini bagels

# Chapter 9:
# ROUND AND ROUND

*Never tell people how to do things. Tell them what to*
*do and they will surprise you with their ingenuity.*

—**GEORGE S. PATTON** (army general)

As I wrote earlier, I usually start my day around 4:00 a.m. At one point, I decided to lead a meditative spinning class every weekday at 5:15 a.m. Selecting this time was a natural decision because I am used to exercising first thing in the morning.

Teaching early made it impossible for the guys at the bakery to call me with problems. Most difficulties happen in the early morning: the oven will not start, the kettle breaks, the refrigerator goes on the blink, there is a flat tire on a delivery vehicle, or someone is late, and so forth.

I wanted a more level playing field, with less dominance from me at the top and more partnering from my "Team Bagel."

I knew the guys would figure things out, but they did not yet know they had the freedom to make decisions with me in charge. After all, my ex had told them what to do for years.

Like I always tell my kids, I tell members of Team Bagel that if there is not a clear rule for how to solve a problem, they should use their best judgment. Often, the solution is not something I would have done; however, allowing others on the team to use their judgment builds trust.

## Spinning Routine

When I lead spinning classes, I put on cycling gear instead of bagel-shop clothes. The gym opens at 5:00 a.m., and my goal is to be there when the door is unlocked.

When I first started teaching, there were zero people in my class. I simply showed up each day, five days a week, and began putting together different rides that complement one another if you do them each day. Gradually, people started to join the class.

Each session begins with meditation. It gently surges from a warm-up into a meditative ride accompanied by a wide range of music and videos.

I always thank everyone for showing up for themselves and for each other. I remind them that if they accomplish nothing else the entire day, they have done this, and that is more than most people think about doing in a day. I tell them this is a community project and we are here for each other. I tell them they have made a huge difference in my life and how much I appreciate them.

After making sure that everyone is properly set up and comfortable on his or her bike, I play gentle music without vocals in a major key—something like solo piano, cello, or guitar. This segment lasts for ten minutes while we get started and focus on the rhythm of our breath.

As our bodies wake up, so do our minds. During the warm-up, we increase resistance on our pedals. Next, I put a video of a tall, white, burning candle on the large screens in the room. The lights are off. I direct everyone to focus on the flame, on breathing, and on the sound of *om*, which is the universal word of oneness used in yoga and meditation.

## Meditation

In spinning class, I have a microphone so I speak gently and can still be heard.

As everyone pedals, I calmly and softly say something like, "Remember that our breath is our inspiration, so breathe deeply and imagine all the qualities you want to bring into your life. As you inhale, bring clarity, peace, contentment, ease, lightness, and gratitude into your experience.

"And as you exhale, soften and release any tightness in your mind and in your body. Notice as you breathe what each breath brings you in its newness. Notice what each breath releases to create space or change. Beautiful…"

Then, a little while later, I will add, "Breathe. Take a moment to be you. Ask yourself, who am I? Where am I going? What do I want to be? Dream… imagine… How do you see yourself five years from now? Imagine how you'll look, what you're wearing, what you're doing… and breathe."

Depending on the ride I have chosen for the day, I will then shift the music to something upbeat and inspiring, like Bob Marley's "Don't Worry, Be Happy." I might use classical music, like Mozart. I have a bassoon concerto that is pretty cool.

If the music does not have an accompanying video, I will play it along with biking videos. We wrap up with a five-minute cool-down period during which I lead an upbeat, motivational stretch with deep breathing and softening of muscles.

I thank everyone for coming, tell them to have a great day, and say I will see them tomorrow. I also ask if anyone needs a wake-up call.

**BAGEL WISDOM**

**ARTISAN BAKERS:** Bakers become experts over time. It takes at least three years to train a baker, depending on the person's inquisitiveness and aptitude. Once trained, a baker can sense the exact weight of a scoop of salt and a cut of yeast (from the one-pound blocks in which ingredients are delivered).

After starting with zero attendance, I now have fifty people who take the class when it is in session. As I always say, "Build it and they will come."

## Prep Process

We open the mixer and pour water, brown sugar, salt, flour, and yeast into it, in that order. The proportion of salt to yeast is important because salt activates yeast. The interaction of salt and yeast affects the dough's ability to rise.

Normally, we weigh the first batch of ingredients on a scale. This tweaks our senses and centers us in the tasks so we can do the rest by touch and feel. Bakers put in thousands of hours; how they blend the ingredients comes through their hearts and souls, becoming second nature to them.

If there's a shift in the weather, bakers must notice it and make adjustments, for temperature affects the rising of the dough. When it is warmer, for example, we add ice to the water before pouring it into the mixture.

We mix the ingredients for 15 minutes. Once the dough is blended, we lift it out of the large mixer and place it onto a stainless steel worktable. We handle more than one hundred pounds of dough at a time. Sometimes we partially cover the dough with plastic and sometimes we do not. It all depends on the weather. The dough is active and will begin to rise if it is too warm.

We use large chef knives to slice the dough into long strips. We then lift each piece onto the top belt of a forming machine, where the dough is fed through a gauge and cut by the machine into rectangular blocks.

The blocks of dough fall onto a lower conveyor belt that gradually curves the pieces into perfect circles and connects the ends. We have calibrated our forming machine so the raw bagels weigh a little over five ounces.

As the now-formed bagels roll off the conveyor belt, either a baker catches them or they fall onto a circular tray from which we pick them up and put them on a board. We ready a stack of boards in advance.

Each board holds thirty-five raw bagels. In the old days, we used wooden boards. I decided to switch to less porous fiberglass because it is easier to clean. Although fiberglass boards are more expensive than wood, they last twice as long. Boards, which get a lot of wear and tear, must be regularly scrubbed and sterilized.

We keep a large bowl of cornmeal nearby so we can grab handfuls to sprinkle onto the fiberglass boards. The cornmeal allows the bagels to slide off the boards into the kettle when we are ready for them.

We place the formed bagels in rows on the boards: seven rows, five bagels per row. They touch each other on all sides as they go through the next steps in the baking process; we call these *kissing bagels*.

I know the conveyor and the large number of bagels makes things sound like the *I Love Lucy* scene in which Lucy and Ethel try to catch quickly moving chocolates on a conveyor belt; however, unlike the comediennes, we have the proper techniques down pat.

Although *boarding* the bagels might look easy when we do it, it takes skill and practice. How the bagels are handled, shaped, and placed on the boards affects how they *proof* (rise) and how we can shape them later. This repetitive work requires alertness and energy.

Thirty-five bagels fit perfectly on a board. This is a little weird, since we count bagels by the dozens and thirty-five is an odd number, but it works.

Previously, we mixed larger batches of dough, but when I downsized the business a few years ago, I scaled down the size of our mixer, too. This means that we must mix, and go through the entire process, more often. I did this so we can better control freshness and consistency.

## Next Steps

Once a board is full, we place it on a rack where the bagels proof for 15 to 20 minutes, depending on the temperature. We look at them, touch them, and decide when they are properly proofed to the point at which we want them.

The bagels rise while they are at room temperature on the racks. There are variables in room temperature; this is where experience and staying alert is vital. If the bagels are neglected, no amount of nurturing can mend them.

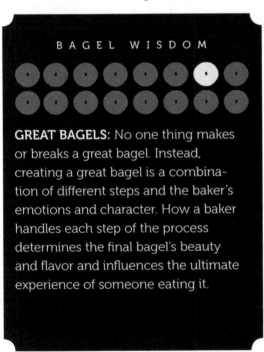

BAGEL WISDOM

**GREAT BAGELS:** No one thing makes or breaks a great bagel. Instead, creating a great bagel is a combination of different steps and the baker's emotions and character. How a baker handles each step of the process determines the final bagel's beauty and flavor and influences the ultimate experience of someone eating it.

Once the bagel dough has risen to our satisfaction, we move the entire rack into the walk-in refrigerator for the bagels to *retard*. Retarding is a second, slower rising of the bagel dough, which happens while it is refrigerated.

We like to retard our bagel dough overnight. This stretches out the fermentation period (the rising) and allows the release of subtle flavors trapped in the flour. Retarding increases the bagel's flavor and gives the crust a deeper color once it is boiled and baked.

This retarding step affects the bagels' texture; if this step is skipped, the bagels are different and have a less intense crust.

Ideally, we let the bagels retard in the refrigerator for twenty-four hours, which allows the proper chemical changes to take place.

After proofing and retarding, we boil bagels for 10 to 60 seconds, depending upon conditions. We retrieve them from the kettle with a large wire scoop, and, shortly thereafter, we bake them in the oven.

We could use automated ways of making bagels, but we craft our products this way to ensure our bagels are the gorgeous, handmade, artisanal creations of which we are so proud.

I love bagels and the process of making them.

# Chapter 10:
# THE SENSUALITY
# OF BAKING

*It has been said that art is a tryst,*
*for in the joy of it maker and beholder meet.*

—**KOJIRO TOMITA** (author)

t is spring. Today, my office is a garden table with an emerald-green umbrella that sits in front of the bagel shop. A
distracting yet heartwarming aspect of this spot is the
smell of bagels that reaches me each time the door swings
open. I am so connected to my business that it is as if the rhythm
of the swinging door matches my heartbeat.

At the moment, the guys are baking bacon on sheet pans in
the oven. The combined smell of bacon and freshly baked bagels
is heavenly. Here on the sidewalk, outside my shop, along with
the literal door to my business, is the figurative door to my home
and my heart. After my struggle to find a home for myself, this
is a comfortable place to be, and it offers me constant adventure.

It is nearly summer. This means that life is slow for bagel
bakers. I feel as though I should be sitting in Northern Michigan,
because that is where I grew up and where I return when I need
to smell pine air, birch trees, and a cool fresh water breeze. It is

where I return when I need stillness, deep sleep, and space to dream.

The sun is up and there is a small but steady stream of bagel-loving customers drifting through the imaginary front door of my bagel office. Everyone says hello as they begin their daily routines.

A regular—a well-groomed man in a suit, dress shirt, and tie—remarks that my office space is civilized. While that is true, I like my office mainly because it suits me.

## Green is a Good Color

The emerald-green umbrellas at the tables in front of the shop are significant. I bought that color because every time I look at the umbrellas, they remind me of my dreams and of the fact that dreams can and do come true. My problem growing up was not about dreaming, but about negating my dreams with the chatter in my head.

*In my experience, dreams come true, but usually not in the way I imagine.*

Since I was a little girl, I have loved emerald stones because of their gorgeous color. I imagined my adult self with a beautiful emerald ring. Although I appreciate the beauty and bling of diamonds, emeralds have always been my favorite.

I have learned to stop negating my dreams and desires; instead, I practice affirming them. In my experience, dreams come true, but usually not in the way I imagine. Often they are better, coming true in more creative ways than I thought possible.

I love the feeling I have when my dreams are realized. These are moments for which I am truly grateful.

After Jonathan and I had lived together for a year, along with our six kids, we decided to get married. One day, Jonathan took me to a jewelry store in Baltimore to pick out an engagement ring. He had not yet proposed officially, but he wanted me to pick out a ring. While I am usually not a jewelry person, I appreciate beautiful things.

I knew Jonathan wanted me to have what I love, so I walked in and asked to see emerald rings. I saw one beautiful emerald set horizontally with a diamond on either side. The ring was simple and gorgeous, and it looked great on my finger. Jonathan walked around the jewelry showroom to catch his breath. Then he bought the ring, which was just like the one that had been in my dreams all those years.

Green is a good color. I use it as much as possible in the bagel shop because it is a reminder for me to stay focused on important things. On St. Patrick's Day, we make green bagels and I give away more than I sell; that is my way of sharing dreams with customers.

BAGEL WISDOM

**DEFINING SUCCESS:**

An artist I know is struggling to determine whether her role as a mother and wife is more meaningful than her art. She is on the verge of realizing she does not have to choose between the two. Nor does she need to feel guilty doing quilting and other projects.

Sometimes going through the motions of less meaningful activities helps us sort out the direction upon which we should focus.

Someone recently asked me if I have a fear of failure. My answer is definitely no, since I am pretty good at dealing with messing up. Success sometimes takes more time to synthesize, but thankfully I am getting more comfortable having things go right for a change.

It has taken hard work, both in my business and my personal relationships, and I believe I have turned a corner.

While I do not yet know what I will find around the next bend, I have earned the self-confidence to know I can handle anything. And when I cannot handle something, I have learned to look to other people who help guide me as I forge my way.

## It is Business, After All:
## Working in the Emerald City

*I have a feeling we're not in Kansas any more.*

**—DOROTHY** to Toto, in The Wizard of Oz

I need to make money to stay in business, but money alone does not represent success for me. I am passionate about bringing happiness to people. For me, business is about more than making money; it is about doing what you love to do.

Around the time I took control of the business, commodity prices skyrocketed, literally doubling. That meant flour prices and most of the other raw ingredient prices doubled.

I did an immediate cost evaluation and raised our bagel price substantially. There was really no choice in my mind because I planned to pay the bills, which could not happen unless our products were properly valued.

Some of my team members have been working at Georgetown Bagelry for fifteen to thirty years. We are a small crew, and we have been together through thick and thin. I pay them well, and they are fantastic at what they do. I never considered paying them less; thus, I had to conduct a proper cost analysis.

Personal satisfaction comes from nurturing a great team, yet the fact remains that numbers are crucial. After all, my responsibility as the company's owner is to ensure we remain strong.

In addition to raising prices, I immediately adjusted our bagels down half an ounce. Reducing the size added up to a lot of dough, and money, saved over the course of a year.

I was learning to make good decisions.

## Making Tough Decisions

At one point, I had to decide what to do with the Georgetown shop. I knew that it would take an enormous amount of time and money to make it a success.

My kids were my priority, and they needed my attention. So I downsized the business, selling the Georgetown location and operating out of Bethesda. I put systems in place, and when the time was right, I got the business growing again.

## Selling to Powerful People

We do not always know how high up our bagels go. However, we did learn that one of the White House chefs was calling for bagels during a Democratic and later a Republican administration.

Secret Service guys came to pick up the bagels; it did not take long for us to figure out the orders were for the White House.

Besides politicians, numerous news media professionals live in, and travel to, the area around our shop, along with actors and other celebrities.

Sometimes celebrities come in the shop. Other times, someone comes in to pick the bagels up for them. We provide bagels to several high-end caterers, too, so our bagels end up in the hands of many recognizable people.

## Living with Consequences

Personal decisions are often more gut-wrenching than business ones.

One of the hardest things I have ever had to do was send my younger son, Badger, to live with one of my brothers and his family for a year and a half.

Badger was fifteen. We were living in a house in D.C. near the border to Maryland. One day, by the grace of God, I picked up a voice message on my cell. I could tell it was Badger's voice, but I could not distinguish what was being said.

I was sure Badger had called by accident and the message was not meant for me. I took my cell phone to the principal of his school. The principal knew right away that the message was gang-related and Badger was headed for trouble.

I staged a sort of intervention. My brother Mike drove down from Michigan and took Badger back with him to live with another of our brothers, who is also named Badger.

Sending Badger to Michigan was one of the hardest things I ever did. He hated me. But I was determined to keep him safe and make sure he was around great men. Luckily for him, and for me, I have great brothers.

## Good and Bad

*One of the very nicest things about life is the way we must regularly stop whatever it is we are doing and devote our attention to eating.*
—LUCIANO PAVAROTTI (opera tenor)

When the kids were growing up, I did not let them watch TV in the morning. Instead, I had them watch classical music videos.

Sometimes, I run those same videos on the TV in the shop. When I stop for a while, customers mention they miss the videos. It is part of our culture to play great music in the shop.

Videos can be good and bad. When he was young, Lucien found his father's videotapes of prostitutes, and he watched them before I did. Lucien did not say much, but I know his father's behavior probably affected him more than it did his siblings, since Lucien was the oldest.

## Bageldom

I guess in some ways, the bagel shop has become my little kingdom of bagels.

One day, I got tired of asking teenagers not to smoke out on the patio where I was working beneath one of the emerald-green umbrellas.

I ordered a danger sign and posted it. The sign reads: DANGER. No Smoking. Bagels Will Blow Up.

People are startled by the sign and point it out to their friends. They even take photos of it with their phones. The sign is a hit. Teenagers get the message and put their smokes away.

While I was on a sign kick, I redid some of the signs in back for the team members—signs reminding them to wash their hands, for instance, and to smile at the customers.

One of my long-time workers crossed out "The Management" from the bottoms of the team signs and replaced it with "Boss Lady." Somehow, that title is sticking, and it seems to be used with affection.

When they heard everyone at the shop using this name, my kids started calling me "Boss Lady," too, in an endearing way.

I seem to attract nicknames, like in law school, when I was known as "The Bagel Lady." People who do not know me well still call me that.

These nicknames are delivered with warmth and I enjoy them. I think of myself now as "Boss Lady" in a gentle, taking-charge kind of way.

## Timing Matters

We bake late at night to be ready for catering and retail sales' early-morning demands. The result of this reality is that most bagel shops close early. We stay open until 10:00 p.m. every day, except Sunday, when we close at 4:00 p.m. (Sunday is our busiest day of the week, even though we close early. It is a huge family day.)

It took several years before customers learned to love having a great bagel sandwich or pizza bagel in the evening. The key to successful evening sales is to always have fresh bagels.

To accomplish this, I make sure there is always a baker managing the shop—one who bakes every few hours.

I also instituted "Bagel Happy Hour" from 6:00 to 10:00 p.m. During this time, all bagels are 50 percent off; sandwiches and other items are still full price.

The shop is set up so people can come in and use the Internet and their laptops. This makes a difference for early-morning and evening business. I encourage writers and students to use the space. It is good to have a positive group of intelligent people around. They support us, and we support them.

# Chapter 11:
# IMPROVING THE BOTTOM LINE

*Making money is art and working is art*
*and good business is the best art.*

—**ANDY WARHOL** (artist)

I take care of myself—mentally, physically, emotionally, and spiritually—doing the daily things I need to do to maintain my equilibrium. There is an ebb and flow to my existence. To prepare for moments when I am not feeling good about myself, I have established a network of people, places, and things that I rely on for support.

The basic things I need to support myself are the following: to be still, eat well, exercise or move, study, journal, surround myself with positive vibrations, and ask for help when I need it.

Most importantly, I need to show up every day. To me, that means facing the conundrums and demons head on. Saying you would really love to do something is meaningless without action. Thinking, voicing, and actually *doing* are different.

Following one's heart can be an important part of a bottom-line equation. In order to be financially successful, people in the arts, and creative people in general, must acknowledge that running a business is more than art.

## Making Big Mistakes

*Saying you would really love to do something is meaningless without action. Thinking, voicing, and actually doing are different.*

An entrepreneur needs a great idea, a sense of adventure, and curiosity, but he or she also needs a great product, financial controls, and marketing.

One great thing that I have gotten from working in the business for so many years is the chance to make mistakes—big mistakes. I learned that this world as I know it does not end when a poor choice is made.

Fortunately, because I continue to focus on creating quality bagels, I have been lucky to enjoy a steady demand and income…even with my mistakes.

## Taking Risks

Being creative means continuously examining what we believe and how we behave.

Mistakes are par for the course when we experiment with new marketing techniques. It is impossible to know the effect of a plan until it is underway.

For example, we tried a group-buying deal in which customers had six months to buy a dozen bagels and a container of cream cheese at half-price. We sold a thousand of these package deals. The last few days of the deal, we were hit with an onslaught of customers who waited until the last minute to come in and get their bagels and cream cheese. That was fine; we could handle the rush.

What was not fine with me was the large number of people who came in after the deadline and begged for their deals to be honored. It was becoming ridiculous. After a day of this craziness, I told my team not to honor the deal past the deadline.

It was easy for me to tell everyone what to do, but I was not the one directly waiting on clients. The whole deal was destroying our team's disposition because we are all uncomfortable saying no to clients. Everyone began to dread the moment when the next person would ask us to recoup the dead deal.

I decided it was not worth gaining the few new people who came into the store because of the deal. It was interesting to do once, but we will not repeat it.

Then there are the changes we implement that lead to great success.... .

## Walking

The secret to a great walk is not thinking about it but just doing it. There is something about putting one foot in front of the other and not stopping for twenty or thirty minutes that changes the way you think and feel about whatever is bothering you.

At any rough time in my life, I walk—not just for the physical benefit, but also for the transformative effect on my mind.

Receiving a good massage works for me too, since it shifts my internal gears and forces me to relax and rest. Shifting the paradigm and doing something completely different, whether it is taking a walk or getting a massage, creates the perfect anxiety reducer. I am much more focused when I do one or both of these simple things.

At one point, I noticed that life was getting sluggish at the shop. Two of the bakers often joked about their ever-growing bellies; they were gaining weight.

I feel that nothing is more unappetizing than going into a restaurant where the employees are overweight. It dawned on me that we might have a win/win situation if everyone on the team had a chance to do something positive for him- or herself while at work.

I wanted everyone who works at the bagel shop to get the personal benefit of taking time alone to walk and think about who they are, where they are going, and what they want to do in life. Moreover, they would get physical benefits from the movement.

The Crescent Trail is a gorgeous wooded path that runs from Bethesda, Maryland, into Washington, D.C., and it passes a half-block from the bagel shop. It made the perfect venue for implementing my idea.

Although we discuss everything as a team, this topic was a hard idea to talk about because no one understood it. It seemed a little crazy to my guys, so the discussion did not go well.

I decided to experiment and put a walking schedule in place without giving anyone a choice. After all, this was gift-giving time. I could not imagine the guys saying no to a great gift. I set the schedule up so each person's walk was scheduled somewhere in the middle of the workday, not at the beginning or end.

A walk shifts a person's consciousness. After taking a walk midday, my workers would come back more consciously present to resume their work. When you do repetitive work, being in a mindful state of consciousness makes a huge difference.

In our case, when we are better we mix, form, board, boil and bake our bagels better. We prepare sandwiches with more attention and serve clients with more joy. Everyone experiences a little more heart and soul.

We are always very busy, so I knew a hard and fast schedule would never work. Even though they did not get the idea at first, my guys made a community effort to figure out who should go for a walk first and when. The team showed that they are made of unlimited creativity. Together, almost anything is possible. Of course, my guys figured it out and had fun doing it.

*In learning to collaborate, we are able to change more than just our bagel shop for the better.*

Occasionally, we have a discussion about whether they are too busy to walk. However, making it happen for each other is important.

In learning to collaborate, we are able to change more than just our bagel shop for the better. We learn to understand and help each other. Then we go home and teach our children, our neighbors, and our communities. This makes for a better world.

## Taking It a Step Further

It became challenging and exciting to support each other's breaks during the day. Each day is different, so the walks happen at different times each day.

The fact that everyone thought I was nuts when we first put this into action makes me grin now, since I was sure there would be great results. I was eager to see the looks on my bakers' faces after they completed their first fifteen walks, because I had decided to implement another reward to their walking routine in addition to the reward of walking itself.

After every fifteen walks, which occurs for each person about once every three weeks, I book the team member an hour-long massage with a great therapist at my cost. Before this, not one person on the team had ever had a massage. Not surprisingly, their gratitude was and is unbelievable.

It gives me great pleasure when I see the team members walking toward the Crescent Trail, where our rule is that no cell phones are to be used. The walk is meant only for reflection and relaxation.

At first, we created a chart, and it became a bit of a competition to see who was walking and who was not. As walking became part of our shop culture, we shifted to having everyone make their own private checklist in a little black writer's book; each person keeps his or hers in a back pocket. After completing fifteen walks, each baker lets me know, and I book the next massage.

Team Georgetown Bagelry is a happy group. In the process of becoming healthier, we have increased efficiency, and the shop has become a happier place for customers, too.

## The Newest Team Member

Toward the end of a new team member's shift, I noticed she seemed a little melancholy and was dragging. Her job is to make great sandwiches and prep food, and I need her to be at her best.

I asked her if she had walked yet that day. She put her head down and shrugged her shoulders. In a nervous way, she said she had too much work to do.

I named three other people who could do what she was doing and told her there were no excuses. Excuses are for another planet. Fair is for our planet, and though these planets are next to each other in outer space, they are different places.

She did not want to go for a walk, and she was unhappy that I did not give her a choice. We had already had all the discussions, so there was no longer going to be any debate as far as I was concerned. This is a healthy choice, like making sure not to touch baked bagels before washing one's hands and using tissue or plastic gloves when handling food. Taking midday walks has become part of who we are at Georgetown Bagelry and how we operate.

Reluctantly, my newest team member bundled up to go outside. It was chilly. A walk alone was daring for her, after all, for she was used to being around other people all the time, whether she was with her husband and children at home or the rest of us at work.

I checked to see if she was leaving her cell phone behind. When I found out she was taking it with her, I temporarily confiscated it. She finally left to take her walk. In the meantime, the rest of us in the shop discussed why no one had noticed she was not walking and encouraged her to take her walks.

I am happy to report that this new worker came back a different person after that first walk. She was smiling and thanked me over and over. I explained that her only responsibility during those twenty-minute walks was to put one foot in front of the other and to think about herself.

When she returned that day (and on subsequent days), she made better sandwiches, was obviously more joyful, and moved around the shop like she had just lost ten pounds.

## Sticking to the Plan

Sometimes the guys will argue that they prefer to take their walks before or after work. However, I am firm about that not being a choice. Walks at other times do not count toward a massage.

When the guys take walks in the middle of the workday, the paradigm shifts. They come back energized and with fresh focus, passion, and ideas.

It is a brilliant thing we have done.

# Chapter 12:
# BAGEL MAGIC

*The bagel is a lonely roll to eat all by yourself because in order for the true taste to come out you need your family. One to cut the bagels, one to toast them, one to put on the cream cheese and the lox, one to put them on the table, and one to supervise.*

—**GERTRUDE BERG,** aka Molly Goldberg (radio personality)

## The History of the "Baker's Dozen"

A baker's dozen is thirteen, occasionally fourteen. The customer buys a dozen and receives the extra bagel or two at no charge.

Bread has long been a staple of life; it is vitally important. Around 1266, England's King Henry III began to enforce an ancient statute, or decree, known as the Assize of Bread and Ale. Bakers (and brewers) who gave what was known as "short measure," or less than was ordered, could be punished, sometimes as severely as losing a hand to an axe.

The decree regulated weight to correspond to the price of wheat rather than the number of loaves. Bakers started adding something extra to make sure the total weight did not accidentally come up short. This way, an extra loaf or two became tradition.

**BAGEL WISDOM**

**AN EXTRA BAGEL GOES A LONG WAY:**
People love a baker's dozen. It is a delightful, generous tradition that never grows old.

While we are bagging their bagels, people smile when we tell them they get an extra bagel free for each dozen they have purchased.

Most customers have heard of a baker's dozen. Still, they forget and are surprised all over again when we ask, "Which bagel would you like for free?" It always brings a spark of joy to people's eyes.

After all, it is a gift, and who does not enjoy that?

This tradition became part of the standard for the Worshipful Company of Bakers—an English guild that regulated the baking profession during medieval times.

While this tradition is traceable to England, it probably occurred in other European countries, too, since shortchanging bread was a serious matter everywhere. Evidence shows that similar issues occurred in ancient Egypt and other societies.

Sometimes we err on the count because it is busy in the store and the customer is telling us, "Give me one of this and two of that." If we lose count or are not sure of the exact amount, we will throw a couple extra in the bag. It is better to give too many than too few.

## Thinking Smart

*The real voyage of discovery consists not in seeking
new landscapes but in having new eyes.*

—**MARCEL PROUST** (author)

I first heard this Proust quote years ago and now I have taken it up as part of my mantra.

Recently, while traveling, I bought bagels in an old-fashioned bagel shop in New England. I was appalled at the way the salesperson waited on me. After rubbing his mouth and nose, he took the bagels from the bins with his bare hands: no paper, no gloves, no nothing.

After touching my money and the cash register, he then waited on the next customer barehanded, again without washing his hands. I stood there in shock, my jaw dropping, because I could not believe what I was seeing. I did not know whether to jump behind the counter to save the customers or not. I could not believe my eyes.

**BAGEL WISDOM**

**FREEZER BAGS:** Team Bagel automatically gives customers freezer bags with orders of four or more bagels. It costs more time-wise to ask someone if he or she wants a bag than the bag costs itself.

To make matters worse, the bagels were underbaked and the dough was old. I was shocked the place was in business.

I encourage my employees to introduce themselves and engage in conversation with customers whether or not the customers buy something. Of course, I insist on hygienic practices—I absolutely insist upon them.

I have heard from numerous customers that they appreciate this accommodation. Small touches like these can make all the difference.

## 50-Percent Military Discount

My older son, Lucien, was in the military. When we were bringing him home from Marine training at Parris Island, South Carolina, we ate lunch in the airport restaurant.

A stranger anonymously paid for Lucien's meal and sent a message saying that he appreciated Lucien's military service. It was profound and touching.

When I got back to the shop, I decided to share this moment with Team Bagel. We immediately initiated a 50-percent discount for everyone active in or retired from the military, and we advertised it through social media marketing.

Men and women who help defend our way of life deserve appreciation. In our small way, we help them by giving a 50-percent military discount. This brings smiles and sometimes tears, especially from older veterans.

It means a great deal to honor these people. We have had many moving conversations with military folks at the bagel shop.

## Hard Moments

Watching my son Lucien, a Marine, go to Iraq was moving, for he looked wonderful and grown-up in his uniform. To me, he is still my small son, and I was terribly nervous seeing him go off to a distant place filled with danger.

I hate to admit it, because it seems unpatriotic, but I was ecstatic when he came back home in one piece. I sleep better now that his tour is over. I would much rather see him carry a violin over his shoulder than a gun.

## "Why Don't You Do-It-Yourself?" Burger Guy

One day, a customer came into the store and placed a fairly large order that included many sandwiches. Among them was a bagel cheeseburger, cooked medium, with cheddar, lettuce, tomato, red onion, and Dijon mustard. It was nothing complicated, but that was *his* sandwich and he wanted it done right.

He repeated his order several times and shouted to the expeditor (the person responsible for making sure the order is completed properly) exactly how to cook the burger on the grill. Then he shouted the same directions to the cook.

I said, "Excuse me, sir, but do you realize that we know exactly what we're doing? The cook has made fifty thousand bagel burgers, and your sandwich is not going to taste any better because you're annoying the hell out of her and making her nervous.

"Why don't you come back here and make it yourself so we can focus on the other 50 people behind you?" I said this in an upbeat way, but the minute it was out of my mouth, I could not believe I had just said what we were all thinking. The man laughed and was quiet. My employees just stared at me and smiled.

I suppose it is ironic I invited a customer to make his own sandwich considering I do not let my husband behind the same counter. It is my business and my baby. Jonathan and I share so much in our lives—six children, two homes, biking, traveling, and talking—yet the back of the bagel shop is my domain. He understands.

## Making a Difference

It is fun having a small business. I am connected to other small business owners who are just as passionate about their companies as I am about mine.

To me, there is nothing more fun than making a difference in the lives of my team members, customers, and vendors—making a difference in the community.

We had a second home in Miami where, for a few years, I spent about a quarter of my time. While I was there, I scouted out bagel shop locations in the downtown area and familiarized myself with the street scene. I worked in the kitchen at Camillus House beside their chef and helped train men working their way off the streets. When I am in Miami now, I work as a volunteer in a homeless shelter's kitchen. I also donate bagels to various charities in D.C. whenever possible. You can never do enough, but we do as much as we can. If a school class, scouting troop, or sports team is having an event, we try to participate, whether it is with a discount or direct donation.

I encourage everyone on Team Bagel to support those less fortunate than they are and to let me know if there is a way Georgetown Bagelry can make a difference.

Luckily, bagels are relatively inexpensive luxuries, so we can make loads of people happy every day.

## Business Decisions

My responsibility as a business owner is to make the bagel shop a strong company. This involves knowing how and when to make decisions.

State government requires that we always have one Food Service Certified person on the premises at all times. I decided to surpass the requirement that one person per shift be certified; instead, I require *all* employees to earn the certification.

This was a challenge to most of my employees, for whom English is a second language. To assist them, I downloaded the materials in different languages, encouraged them to study together in pairs during breaks, and later hired a bilingual instructor to come in and train the team.

*One bagel at a time—and one employee at a time: this saying exemplifies how I am developing my business.*

As a result, the entire team knows the rationale behind the systems we use, and having this knowledge boosts their self-esteem.

I have always been certified, but it does not do much good if I am not there when the health department comes in. My managers have always been certified, too. Now, the health department treats us like gold because we broke the mold. It was not difficult.

Food Service Certification is money well spent. It actually cost less to have everybody do it at the same time.

One bagel at a time and one employee at a time—this saying exemplifies how I am developing my business.

# Chapter 13:
# SERENDIPITY

*We don't see things as they are, we see things as we are.*

—**ANAÏS NIN** (author)

## Classic

A really fresh bagel is good by itself, or with cream cheese and perhaps a bit of smoked salmon, and maybe with a slice of tomato or red onion.

It does not take much to dress up a bagel because it is delicious in and of itself. It may already be dressed up on its own with sesame or poppy seeds, onion, garlic, or salt.

Bagels are baked in a distinctive shape and size. Each bagel should be eaten by one person. Of course, a bagel can be shared, but generally a bagel lands on a person's plate and is all his or hers.

The rather funny look of a bagel—after all, it has a hole in the middle—invariably brings smiles to its recipient. A bagel is fun to eat because of its shape, texture, and unique taste.

That is enough for most people.

## Innovative

We love doing new things.

We welcome new ideas for product development with the understanding that each new product needs to be more than fun; it must also be profitable.

Most of our specialty items come from playing with the bagel dough, or as ideas from conversations with each other and our customers.

We talk a lot in the bagel shop. Behind the scenes, we sing, we dance, and we hug each other when we need it. It is a great place to be creative.

*Behind the scenes, we sing, we dance, and we hug each other when we need it.*

## The "No Hole" Lady

One day, we had a customer who asked us to make platters of bagels cut in quarters—not sliced in half first and then quartered, simply quartered. She was having lady friends over to play cards and thought this would be the perfect thing. She was eccentric, wealthy, and a regular customer.

All we could think about was how dry the quartered bagels would be by the end of the day. However, there was no talking her out of it. She did not want mini bagels, because she does not like bagel holes. She wanted her bagels cut up.

We did what she asked, but the sandwich pieces were awkward and the platters looked weird. We decided to come up with something better.

We experimented by taking a chef's knife and quartering the bagels before we put them in the kettle. That gave each piece of bagel a beautiful little crust and glossy appearance. The pieces still had the slight curve of a bagel, but they were without holes.

However, there were too many little pieces to place on boards to bake; plus, we were burning our hands trying to take them off the boards. It was ridiculous to have fifty zillion bagel pieces peeling out of the oven, with some falling to the bottom of the oven and burning up.

The bagel pieces needed seeds on both sides, and they needed to be baked on both sides. No one would want anything half-baked.

We figured the most efficient way to bake little pieces would be on sheet pans with baking paper so they did not stick. The little bagel pieces bake differently than a whole bagel does because a little piece has less surface area.

*One of my favorite tweets on Twitter is, "Tweets are to Twitter as teasers are to bagels!" Social media buffs love it.*

These bagel sections turned out to be absolute nuggets from heaven. They are bite-sized pieces that are chewy and manageable. They contribute to beautiful platters and taste much better than quartered bagels.

Next, these little buggers needed a name. We put them in a wicker basket on top of the bagel display case, and everyone who walked into the shop saw them. Customers started calling them by different names: "bagel holes," "nuggets," "pieces," and "midgets." It got confusing and became a tease, so I made an executive decision and decided to use "teasers." No one else was making them, and I trademarked the name.

One of my favorite tweets on Twitter is, "Tweets are to Twitter as teasers are to bagels!" Social media buffs love it.

We give teasers to little kids so they are happy while they wait in line with their parents.

**BAGEL WISDOM**

**STICK-WICHES:** My son Badger had the great idea of making bagel stick sandwiches. The next menu we print will have them as a regular item. We call them "stick-wiches."

Stick-wiches are oddly shaped, since the sandwich surface is long and narrow, making them hard to slice. They are winners, though, because they are easy to eat.

## Magic Wands

We created bagel sticks when a restaurant's employees asked us to supply an item that would fit into their wicker breadbaskets. Now we make two sizes of bagel sticks: five-ounce versions and two-and-a-half-ounce versions.

To create a five-ounce bagel stick, we take a formed raw bagel, cut it, and roll it straight on a bread table. To create two small bagel sticks, we cut each formed raw bagel twice and roll the pieces straight. As we do with teasers, we bake these sticks on sheet pans for manageability.

The large bagel sticks are almost like clubs or swords, so we have fun playing with them. Occasionally, we will poke each other with one or playfully slap someone if they have done something stupid (not hard, just for fun).

The little sticks come in handy as "magic wands." Whenever we have an unhappy child in the shop, a magic wand comes alive. It is rare when we cannot make a child smile.

If one of the bakers is having an off day, I twirl a wand over his or her head and sprinkle magic bagel fairy dust. It makes everyone laugh and helps change thinking.

Bagel sticks truly bring happiness to those in need of an attitude adjustment.

## Miami Burgers

There are many bagel lovers in Miami, Florida, including one who travels to our shop whenever he is in the area. He regularly orders an everything bagel filled with cream cheese, lox, tomato, and fresh red onion, and he calls it a "Miami Burger." The name has stuck; now, it is our most popular sandwich.

For customers who ask, we will scoop out part of the bagel so the crust is still there, providing the taste without too many carbs or calories.

The *burger* part is misleading, since there is no ground meat. However, once customers taste it, they fall in love with the sandwich. It is no wonder. The sandwich is out-of-this-world delicious, as if from another planet.

## Pregels

Shaped like a pretzel and hand-molded from bagel dough, what we call "pregels" are a hit, especially with children. We use kosher salt on them, and customers dip them in honey mustard.

Like us, many bakeries in Long Island and Northern New Jersey are now producing pregels.

## Flagels

Another one of our novelties is a flat bagel that uses the same amount of dough as a bagel but has more surface area and crunchiness.

In New York City, flagels are called "flats." We call them "flagels," combining the words *flat* and *bagel,* and we make them in both full-size and minis.

Both sizes are made using a special stainless steel bagel flattener we created called "the smasher." We make wonderful pizza flagels and awesome open-faced sandwich melts.

It is difficult to look at a flagel and not think, "Frisbee." They are fun to hold, and sometimes we toss them around to each other (naturally, we trash the ones we throw). If your Frisbee skills are good, you have flagel potential.

We have fun. There are few dull moments in the bagel shop.

## Happiness Bagels

A while back, I asked all my followers on Facebook to tell me about their favorite bagel sandwiches. I announced that the winner of the most creative sandwich would get a bagel hat (a baseball cap with our logo embroidered on it).

A little girl named Liza told us she loves a pumpernickel bagel loaded with smashed avocado and sprinkled with sesame seeds, sea salt, and freshly squeezed lemon juice. She easily won the contest.

Inspired by Liza, I decided to create a special bagel for happiness. After experimenting, we ended up with a pumpernickel, sesame, and salt bagel. It is awesome.

Periodically, I will announce on Facebook that if a customer comes in with a copy or download of a particular book I mention that day, that person will receive a free happiness bagel.

*You can spread too much cream cheese, but you cannot spread too much happiness.*

You can spread too much cream cheese, but you cannot spread too much happiness.

## No, They're Not Bagels

Years ago, we stopped mixing special dough for *bialys* to save time, since we were not selling many. There was a reason they were not selling: they were not very good.

Bialys were always an afterthought for us. Recently, we had time to tweak the original recipe. This means we no longer use the same dough for bialys as we do for bagels.

Now we mix bialy dough in a small mixer three to four times a week (sometimes more, depending on surges in business). We blend chopped, dried onion into the bialy dough and mix it five minutes longer than bagel dough.

We cut the dough into two-ounce portions and round it into balls before we proof it. We proof bialys longer than bagels, and we put more water in the bialy dough.

With the first batch, we go ahead and form as many as we need for that day. We form them between our hands, using our fingertips to gently caress and knead the dough.

**BAGEL WISDOM**

**BIALYS:** Bialys are a flat bread roll topped with carmelized chopped onions, poppy seeds, and garlic.

Bialy is a Yiddish word short for *bialys-toker küchen,* from Bialystock, a city in Poland. It's an old bread term which is new to many Americans.

We brush flour on the table and use it on our hands to help handle the dough. It is important not to use too much flour—just enough to easily form the bialys.

We chop fresh onions and caramelize them on the ledge of a hot oven until they brown. The mixture we place in the center of each bialy is made of these fresh caramelized onions, poppy seeds, and garlic. We bake the bialys directly on one of the stone shelves in the oven; we do not use a pan or burlap board.

It is amazing how recipes and baking processes morph over time. Sometimes changes happen organically, in a natural and productive way. Other times, it is important to notice when something is not working, as we did with the bialys. Once we notice, we can make changes and corrections.

## Planning or Winging It

One day, while Badger was delivering bagels in the bagel mobile—a small car that we retrofitted to deliver bagels and publicize the shop—he hit a deer.

Somewhere in D.C., a wounded deer was running around wrapped in bagels. The big deer was actually fine, but the bagel mobile went through a painful makeover to fix the damage and make it better than ever.

It is never dull around here.

BAGEL WISDOM

**SERENDIPITY AND KARMA:**

I am letting the universe speak to me.

I love clarity. Often, I can be with other people and inspire them. It is just how I am. I speak, and people seem to listen.

When I play music, it is the same. Even when I am dancing or baking, I have learned to step outside myself and let the beauty be what it is. This beauty is most easily expressed through art forms.

I love ideas. Writing my ideas clearly makes me feel more full of meaning. The more I interact with artistic individuals, the stronger I feel my own calling to write become.

# Chapter 14:
# FULL CIRCLE

*There are two ways to live: you can live as if nothing is a miracle; you can live as if everything is a miracle.*

—**ALBERT EINSTEIN** (physicist)

I have streamlined the bagel bakery business to become efficient and to maximize production. As I described earlier, I downsized the business by selling the Georgetown location and concentrated all my efforts in the Bethesda shop. I purchased a small mixer so we would have to mix dough more often, improving freshness and consistency.

My marketing activities were nonexistent until I discovered social media. In one week, I made more progress in marketing my bagel business than I had in the previous 20 years.

## Internet Marketing

Besides the social marketing that I do through Twitter, Facebook, Pinterest, Foursquare, and Yelp, my team also takes orders via e-mail, our website, and our mobile app.

One favorite client of mine owns a coffee shop. He sends his daily order to me via e-mail each night, along with a cheerful and funny comment. "We wish for rounded goodness on our doorstep tomorrow morn," he will write, along with an order for six dozen various bagels.

Alternatively, he will order eight dozen bagels of various types, along with a note that says, "Bagel me, please," "Our bins are empty and we hunger for more," or, "We would love some baaaagels."

Sometimes this customer places an order for seven-and-a-half dozen bagels and signs off with, "Bagels away." Two of my favorite slogans are "We have a bagel deficit" and "We have the hunger: the hunger for bagels."

Not only is this man an excellent customer, he is clever. Receiving his order each night is a pleasure.

**BAGEL WISDOM**

**SAMPLE TWEETS @GtownBagel:**

Good morning, good morning, good morning...

Fresh baked sesame bagels! Did you know there's calcium in sesame seeds?

More hot bagels! Cinn/raisin, plain, poppy, ET, sesame

Winner receives FREE Baker's Dozen! Name this platter.

Hot mini bagels! Check out our mini menu; entire menu on minis.

We're heading into HAPPINESS HAPPENS MONTH! Guess which bagel is our happiness bagel & guess why www.facebook.com/GTBagel

## On a Roll... or Better Yet, a Bagel

I am often asked what it takes to make a really good bagel. After all, bagels are much more than pieces of bread with holes.

Fresh is best, which is why we mix our dough only as we need it. Temperature of the air and water matters, as does the type of yeast, flour, and sugar the baker uses.

BAGEL WISDOM

**FILLING IN THE HOLES:** It is a great thing to be surrounded by passionate people like the members of my team. This does not happen as if by magic. We build trust and a code of communication that works regardless of where we start and the native language we speak.

It is best not to use preservatives—only pure ingredients. You need experience, of course; the best bagels are handcrafted, and you need to think about what you are doing. The great bakers put their hearts and spirits into their work.

Then magic happens. We have managed to capture that magic at Georgetown Bagelry and become a mecca for bagel lovers in our area. There is usually a line out the door and into the parking lot because our bagels are, well, great.

I have worked hard to make that happen. So has the rest of my team.

## How My Life Parallels My Business

There are various forms of resistance in my life—resistance to face my fears, resistance to change, and resistance to almost anything and everything if I allow it—but I no longer permit doubts to hamper my success.

Yet I recognize that my business does not define me. It is a vehicle to make money, it is an outlet for my creativity, it is a way to express my feelings for other people—whether they are employees, customers, or suppliers—and it represents the enjoyment that comes from accomplishment.

However, I know in my heart that there is more to me than business. That is only part of who I am.

Although I choose not to separate what I do for a living from who I am, there are different versions of my "truth."

## Confessions of a Bagel Lady

In a desire for full disclosure, I want to reveal that in this book I call my first husband "Razz," which is not his real name. Like most former spouses, I rarely use my ex-husband's actual name.

Once relationships end, many of us refer to our former "other" as "my ex," "he," or something derogatory. Instead of those terms, I am choosing to call my ex-husband "Razz." Like *razzmatazz*, which is flashy action designed to deceive, my first husband was all surface glitter. The name certainly fits.

As a result of our marriage, I have three wonderful children. Life with Razz was difficult, to say the least, and it was even dangerous many times. However, something precious—my children—came from the trauma that frequented my marriage.

My children faced a great deal of stuff when they were younger, and I did not hide anything from them, for I felt I owed them honesty. I felt it was particularly important that they learn to understand their father's addictive behavior. I am proud of my children because they love their father in spite of his shortcomings; they are respectful of him, too.

My bagel business, which I would never have had if not for Razz, is my other pride and joy. Yet if I had left the business with him, it never would have survived. Georgetown Bagelry lasted, and now thrives, thanks to the love and energy I give to the business.

*I believe that my management style, which includes viewing my employees as partners, helps foster Georgetown Bagelry's success.*

I believe that my management style, which includes viewing my employees as partners, helps foster Georgetown Bagelry's success. These individuals, upon whom I depend, give me a major advantage.

## Bagel Chips (My Kids) Off the Old Block (Me)

I am proud of my children for many reasons, and I am especially thankful they each got to know my mother, who was a truly loving woman. I am honored to be her daughter.

After Mom died, my family planned a memorial service in Michigan. This service happened a month after she passed away, since we had to arrange for family to attend from all over the country.

It was not a religious service. Instead, everyone who wanted to participate got up to talk about Mom. I told my kids, "This is it. There are no repeats."

I was proud of each one of them. My daughter, Retha, is her grandmother's namesake, and she wrote her own remarks. I could not help but cry when she got up and told everyone, "When I was younger, Grandma Retha held *my* hand. Then, when she was older, I held *her* hand."

She looked up, as if talking directly to her grandmother, and said, "God loves you and so do I," which is something my mother always said. My daughter added, "I am here to say that Team Retha continues."

It has been several years, but last month my daughter posted this on Facebook: "I miss my Grandma Retha and her gentle ways. I am glad my mom's hugs feel like hers did. Miss you Grandma... Team Retha is still in full effect."

Some memories are priceless.

## Cream Cheese of Life

*One cannot think well, love well, sleep*
*well, if one has not dined well.*

—VIRGINIA WOOLF (author)

## Things Do Not Always Go Smoothly

My son Lucien is great with numbers. Perhaps it is his military training, or it may be an innate ability. When we had glitches in our point-of-sale (POS) system, Lucien found the source of the problem.

When we lost power for several days after a major storm, I asked him to help and he showed up immediately. And when I broke my arm in a biking accident, he stood by my side and worked the front counter on Yom Kippur—our busiest night—

when customers pick up their orders after fasting and praying for twenty-four hours.

That night, both my sons stepped in and helped me with the orders. They helped people carry large trays out to their cars. They did whatever I asked and whatever was needed. We were exhausted from baking so much more than usual, and I was frustrated that I could not use my arm.

My sons came to the rescue.

**BAGEL WISDOM**

**RECIPE FOR CONTENTMENT:**

Lately, I have been going to the shop at 3:30 in the morning, and I am exhausted. However, I am having a hard time slowing down because everything I am doing is so much fun.

I changed the bagel mix when the weather changed, and I love being there when the first bagels roll out of the oven. There is truly nothing like it, and the bagels have never been better.

## Conversation

At one point, my son Badger began working for me on a full-time basis. One day, Badger came outside and sat down under the emerald-green umbrella with me because he wanted to talk. We sat quietly for a little while, since I wanted to let him find his words. Most of my meaningful conversations happen when I am hanging out in front of the bagel shop in my homemade office.

Badger said, "Mom, I think you know your employees better than you know me."

I had to think about what he said for a minute. I took a deep breath and chose my words carefully. "Well, Badge, you know, you're right. They probably *do* know me better in some ways because we've been together longer.

*There is always something to learn. Conversations and dialogues are where we bridge gaps and build understanding.*

"I don't know about knowing them 'better' than you; my relationship with them is *different* from the one I have with you. Many of us were together way before you were born.

"One of these women and I worked together throughout our first pregnancies with big bellies, side by side, until we delivered. That was when I was pregnant with your older brother.

"Two of the men have been here thirty years, and you are only twenty. I have been through rough times with the people who work here, and we've shown up for each other when no one else would or could. We look at each other and sense what's going on because we know many of each other's subtleties.

"Even though several of my employees speak different languages, we've learned to communicate using our eyes, hands, and anything else we can think of using. We know each other well as a result, and we keep learning to communicate better.

"We have a long history of trust, Badger, and that did not happen by accident. It took time and conscious effort."

When I finished, he nodded his head with a smile. Conversations like these are so important and should not be taken for granted. I am glad my son came to me with his observations, since this turned into an important dialogue for both of us.

One of my personal goals is to keep the conversation going with everyone who matters to me. There is always something to learn. Conversations and dialogues are where we bridge gaps and build understanding.

I find it amazing that when we understand why someone thinks or does something differently from what we would think or do in the same situation, we find similarities or at least learn to appreciate our diversity. We find that we are not so different after all; we can work together and create something awesome.

# Food for Thought

A smile, a moment in nature, the time to savor a wonderful bagel—this is what I want to pass on to others.

That is at the heart of who I am.

The joy starts by anticipating the taste and enjoying the smell.

It may be as simple as snacking on a plain bagel with cream cheese.

Alternatively, you can create an enticing bagel sandwich.

You can pair a bagel with an omelet or salad.

You may want to toast the bagel, slicing it first.

Or you can break the bagel up and eat it in little pieces.

Imagine scooping it out and filling it with everything you love.

It is all up to you.

*"I suppose I ought to eat or drink something or other;
but the great question is, what?"*

—**LEWIS CARROLL,** Alice in Wonderland

*"Bagels, of course. Nothing is better!
There's even meaning in the holes."*

—**MARY BEALL ADLER**

# About the Author

Mary Beall Adler is a bagel baker, entrepreneur, creativity coach, mother, wife, and seeker of truth. Her personal journey has been filled with twists and turns she never anticipated. She overcame adversity, which led her to become more reflective, more spiritual, and increasingly interested in sharing what she learned.

As a mother, Mary is nurturing, and as a bakery owner, she is responsible for baking and selling nurturing food. To get there, Mary had to learn self-sufficiency. Never one to sit out a dance, she took risks and made some questionable choices before she learned to discern the right path and the right people who would help her thrive.

Mary owns Georgetown Bagelry, a retail and wholesale bakery in the upscale Bethesda suburb of Washington, D.C. Besides managing the business, Mary works alongside her employees in the hard but satisfying work of baking artisanal bagels. Through this craft, she has learned to make positive choices and create authentic products using hands, head, and heart.

Mary is happy with her second husband, Jonathan, and her business is thriving, as are the six children of their blended marriage.

Not one to rest on her laurels, while continuing to run Georgetown Bagelry, Mary has started a second business as a creativity coach to other entrepreneurs, artists, and athletes. She actively volunteers her time to D.C.'s Bread for the City and Miami's Camillus House for the Homeless.

Prior to running her businesses, Mary earned her B.A. in English Literature from the University of Maryland, College Park, and attended Antioch Law School for two years. While education is obviously important to her, much of what she relays in this book was learned from the school of hard knocks.

Mary enjoys cycling, practicing yoga, walking, meditating, reading, playing piano, and sharing inspiring ideas through social media. A former gymnast and elite coach with expertise in choreography, Mary is also an accomplished dancer, and she teaches meditative spinning.

## Mary Beall Adler

CEO, Georgetown Bagelry

7804 Westfield Drive

Bethesda, MD 20817

202-230-2117 (mobile)

mary@georgetownbagelry.com

For more information, please visit Mary's websites:

GeorgetownBagelry.com

MaryBeallAdler.com